# TRANSACTIONS

*of the*

## American Philosophical Society

*Held at Philadelphia for Promoting Useful Knowledge*

VOLUME 82 Part 2

# Francis Bacon
# and
# Scientific Poetry

## Robert M. Schuler

THE AMERICAN PHILOSOPHICAL SOCIETY

Independence Square, Philadelphia

1992

Library of Congress Catalog
Card Number 91-76985
International Standard Book Number 0-87169-822-6
US ISSN 0065-9746

# CONTENTS

# ACKNOWLEDGMENTS

Thanks are due to Patrick Grant for a helpful critique of an earlier version of Part II, and to the President's Committee on Faculty Research and Travel, University of Victoria, for making possible some of the research for this study.

I am grateful to the following publishers for the use of copyright material that is here reprinted by permission: The University of Chicago Press for Benjamin Farrington, *The Philosophy of Francis Bacon* (1964); Harvard University Press for Lucretius, *De Rerum Natura*, trans. W. H. D. Rouse, rev. Martin Ferguson Smith (1975); and The Johns Hopkins University Press for Eva M. Thury, "Lucretius' Poem as a *Simulacrum* of the *Rerum Natura*," *American Journal of Philology*, 108 (1987).

# I. INTRODUCTION: POETRY, KNOWLEDGE, AND SCIENTIFIC POETRY

In the "ancient quarrel between philosophy and poetry" (*Republic* 607b)—ancient already to Plato and still with us—a major, recurring conflict has been that between the didactic and the mimetic. In both the *Apology* and *Ion* Plato queried the traditional association between poetry and knowledge, and he debunked the encyclopedic learning that some found in Homer. Against his assertion in the *Republic* that epic and tragedy merely "imitate" the life of visible nature which was itself only a pale reflection of the perfect world of Forms, Aristotle replied that such poetry is "more philosophical and a higher thing than history" in its ability "to express the universal" which transcends the "particular" facts of history (*Poetics* 51a36–51b7). But he still accepted his teacher's implicit definition of poetry as imitation and therefore minimized its claim to be "knowledge." Poetry may be "more philosophical" than history, but it is still not philosophy, its "universality" being confined to human events that illustrate "how a person of a certain type will on occasion speak or act, according to the law of probability or necessity." Even to claim this much for poetry, however, Aristotle had to construct definitions so rigid that he himself had difficulty adhering to them.

At the very beginning of the *Poetics* he sets out his criterion of mimesis and immediately applies this touchstone to Empedocles:

when a treatise on medicine or natural science is brought out in verse, the name of poet is by custom given to the author; and yet Homer and Empedocles have nothing in common but the meter, so that it would be right to call the one poet, the other physicist rather than poet (47b16–20).[1]

---

[1] Translations of the key terms vary slightly; I have been citing S. H. Butcher, *Aristotle's Theory of Poetry and Fine Art*, 4th ed. (London: Macmillan, 1907), 9. The Loeb ed. reads, "medical or scientific treatises . . . not a poet but a scientist"; Alan H. Gilbert translates, "If a writer presents medicine or natural philosophy in meter . . . the one is justly called a poet, but the other should be called a natural philosopher" (*Literary Criticism Plato to Dryden*, ed. Gilbert [New York: American Book Co., 1940], 70); and Gerald F. Else offers, "If they [writers] put out some medical or scientific work in verses, . . . the proper thing is to call the one a poet, the other a scientific writer" (*Aristotle's Poetics: The Argument* [Cambridge, Mass.: Harvard University Press, 1957], 39–40).

1

In an earlier work, however, where mimesis is apparently not the *sine qua non* of poetry, Aristotle had found Empedocles and Homer to share much more. He admiringly speaks of Empedocles as "of Homer's school and powerful in diction, being great in metaphors and in the use of all other poetic devices."[2] This judgment of Empedocles' poetic gifts (in particular his ability to create powerful similes and metaphors) is closer to that of Plutarch and—as Kirk, Raven, and Schofield suggest—to that of most readers since. No mere versified scientific treatise, Empedocles' philosophical and scientific speculations on the nature of reality are seen as gaining from his decision to write in figurative language and poetic form.[3]

But even in the *Poetics*, where the mimetic theory demanded that hexameters do not a poet make and where Empedocles' scientific subject matter is theoretically rejected, it is clear that Aristotle thought of Empedocles both "by custom" (as a poet) and with great fondness: he cites Empedocles more than any other writer, whether poet or philosopher, except Homer and Plato. To account for this, it has been argued that Aristotle valued Empedocles' style (most of the citations in *Poetics* have to do with his figurative language, prosody, etc.) while not accepting his subject matter. But as Gerald F. Else points out (agreeing with Aristotle in *On Poets* and with Plutarch and others), Empedocles is more than "a great stylist or a Homeric hand with a metaphor," and such an explanation does not satisfy our sense of discrepancy. He re-

---

[2] *On Poets*, in a fragment preserved in Diogenes Laertius, *Lives of Eminent Philosophers*, 8, 57; trans. R. D. Hicks, 2 vols. (London: Heinemann, 1950), II, 373.

[3] G. S. Kirk, J. E. Raven, and M. Schofield, *The Presocratic Philosophers: A Critical History with a Selection of Texts*, 2nd ed. (Cambridge: Cambridge University Press, 1983), 283–84. See also the remarkable similes (which are actually scientific analogies based on careful observation, e.g., of a household vessel working on the principle of a pipette) preserved by Aristotle in fragments 389, 471; and frags. 355 and 356 for Empedocles' "empirical modes of argument" (293–94).

Perhaps the most important classical appreciation of Empedocles comes from another scientific poet, Lucretius. For him, *poetry* is what clarifies the sometimes obscure teachings of his master Epicurus (who, ironically, thought the medium of poetry inadequate to philosophy). To make his point, Lucretius confronts directly the problem of philosophical and scientific language in Book I of *De rerum natura* and contrasts the precision of Empedocles' poetry with the vagueness of the prose of Heraclitus and Anaxagoras. Empedocles is "*praeclarus* and his glory is his *carmina*." Using the imagery of light/dark for reason/ignorance, Lucretius asserts (1.921–950) that "poetry is the medium of . . . *ratio*" and is itself "a vehicle of pellucid exposition . . . Thus Lucretius' praise for Empedocles, motivated by his admiration for the Sicilian's verse, reflects the Roman's conscious belief, stated openly several times, that poetry is well able to communicate philosophical ideas understandably." See Jeffrey W. Tatum, "The Presocratics in Book One of Lucretius' *De rerum natura*," *Transactions of the American Philological Association* 114 (1984), 177–89; quotations from 186, 187.

gretfully concludes that Aristotle's exclusion of didactic poetry (however imaginatively powerful or linguistically rich) and his insistence that poetry deal only with men and men's actions reveal "the limitations of Aristotle's philosophy and aesthetic capacity."[4]

If the exclusivity of the mimetic theory reveals its first systematic formulator's ambivalence and a consequent disjunction—if not outright self-contradiction—in his argument, such confusion was also one of the less happy legacies of the *Poetics* for later ages.[5] The Renaissance, with its rediscovery of ancient science (which included among others the scientific poems of Xenophanes, Empedocles, Parmenides, Lucretius, and the *Georgics* of Virgil), saw both a renewal of the old debate over the mimetic-didactic distinction and a widening of the ambiguity and confusion in Aristotle. Before turning to the debate itself, in which Francis Bacon was a reluctant but important participant, I should perhaps explain the term "scientific poetry," which I apply to the works of those writers just named.[6] Like many terms in genre criticism, this one is formulated after the fact, and I am fully aware that my attempts at definition are likely to be no more successful than Aristotle's. There are, however, reasons both practical, logical, and historical for adopting such a term.

First, while classicists have long used *Lehrgedicht* to designate any didactic or non-mimetic poem whose main purpose is to teach, it is necessary to distinguish between those didactic poems of antiquity that attempt to describe or explain the workings of the natural world or our perception of it (via metaphysical, cosmological, and epistemological speculation or through observation of the physical universe) from those didactic poems on such subjects as conduct in social and religious life (Hesiod, *Theogony*), hunting (Grattius "Faliscus," *Cynegetica*), or the art of poetry (Horace). The most important poems for the later history of di-

---

[4]*Aristotle's Poetics: The Argument*, 51; for a full discussion of Aristotle's inconsistency and his ambivalence toward Empedocles, see 50–53. W. Hamilton Fyfe, the Loeb translator of *Poetics*, remarks that while "Aristotle elsewhere attributes genuine value as poetry [to Empedocles' scientific poetry], . . . it is here excluded from the ranks of poetry because the object is definitely didactic" (p. 8 n. *a*).

[5]For a survey of the earlier period, see Robert M. Schuler and John G. Fitch, "Theory and Context of the Didactic Poem: Some Classical, Mediaeval, and Later Continuities," *Florilegium* 5 (1983), 1–43, on which some of these introductory remarks are based.

[6]I would also include Hesiod's *Works and Days* and the Hesiodic *Astronomy*, Nicander, Aratus, Manilius, Columella (Book X of *De re rustica* is in hexameters), the Byzantine alchemical poet Heliodorus, and Oppian, as well as the Latin verse translations of Aratus' *Phaenomena* by Cicero, Germanicus, and Avienus.

dactic poetry were those on scientific subjects, and their critical
problems have always been greater. (The terms "philosophical"
and "didactic," though both are usable in certain contexts, also
carry associations that are potentially misleading.) Besides, in the
*locus classicus* of the didactic-mimetic debate, Aristotle refers to
Empedocles as a "physicist" whose subjects are "medicine or
natural science," and this reference (rather than, say, his later
distinction between a hypothetical versification of Herodotus'
history and mimetic poetry) was the flash point for most later
contention over mimetic-didactic.[7]

Second, while some of these poems obviously contain narrative, "mimetic" elements (e.g., the Iphigenia story or the plague
of Athens sequence in *De rerum natura* 1.80–101, 6.1138–1286; or
the Aristaeus epyllion in *Georgics* 4) and while some at times
verge on theology (Xenophanes) or theogony (Parmenides), a
major concern in all of them is man's attempt to explain or
(thereby) to manipulate the physical world.[8] Third, for centuries
they were perceived as having practical (i.e., technical) and scientific value. It is primarily for their applicability to natural
philosophy—what we broadly call "science," including pre-
modern "proto-science"—that such poems were prized in the
Renaissance, the period whose appropriation of them I am here
attempting partly to reconstruct. Bacon (whom we anachronistically call a "philosopher of science" but who called his subject
"philosophy" or "natural philosophy") is only the most celebrated scientific writer thus to make use of them. Finally, "scientific poetry" is the best modern equivalent for the term
"philosophical poetry" as used by Renaissance literary humanists, both those who wrote scientific poems inspired by the
ancients (poems—Neo-Latin and vernacular—on astronomy,
medicine, biology, meteorology, natural history, and mathemat-
ics, as well as on astrology and alchemy), and those who theo-
rized about this kind of didactic. Faced with the awkward fact

[7]Of course, historical poetry had its own struggle for legitimacy; see Wyman H. Heren-
deen, "Wanton Discourse and the Engines of Time: William Camden—Historian among
Poets-Historical," *Renaissance Rereadings: Intertext and Context*, ed. Maryanne Cline Horo-
witz et al. (Urbana: University of Illinois Press, 1988), 142–56.

[8]Not even in the case of Xenophanes "is it safe to exaggerate his non-scientific character
on the grounds of his theological interest; the study of gods was not divorced from that of
nature, and the deduction from fossils [cited on pp. 177f.], whether or not it reflects
original observation, shows careful and by no means implausible argument from observed
fact to general hypothesis—a procedure notoriously rare among the Presocratics" (Kirk
et al., *Presocratic Philosophers*, 168). Mythography, of course, had its place even in Bacon,
and his works are permeated with scriptural references and theological concerns, despite
his insistence that science and divinity must be kept separate.

that no separate name had been given to this genre in antiquity, they provided one; in so doing, they effectively reconstituted the genre for the Renaissance.[9] If it had not existed, they would have had to invent it.

We can now turn to the mimetic-didactic dispute which scientific poetry set off among the Italian humanists.[10] Here the controversy raged not only over the Stagirite's test case, Empedocles, but also over Virgil, Lucretius, and especially Dante, who had incorporated a good deal of abstract teaching (science, philosophy, theology) in his poems. Among the stricter Aristotelians, who rejected scientific poetry because it failed to be mimetic, were Sperone Speroni, Benedetto Varchi, Ludovico Dolce, Pier Vettori, Bernardino Partenio, Antonio Minturno, and Tasso. On the other side were the "anti-Aristotelians," those who rejected mimesis as a *sine qua non* and who were unequivocally in favor of scientific poetry: Francesco Patrizi, Bernardino Tomitano, and J. C. Scaliger (though the latter was considered an arch-Aristotelian by later critics). Patrizi was able to find support for the scientific poets of antiquity in the praise accorded them by Cicero, Quintilian, and Horace; this approbation was in turn used to validate contemporary Neo-Latin poems inspired by the ancient originals such as Pontano's *Urania* and Fracastoro's *Syphilis*. But Patrizi carried his disagreement with Aristotle so far as to exalt Empedocles above Homer.

---

[9]See, e.g., the edition of the Presocratic poetic fragments by Sir Philip Sidney's friend, Henri Estienne: *Poesis philosophica vel saltem reliquiae poesis philosophicae, Empedoclis, Parmenidis, Xenophanis* . . . (Geneva, 1573). Implicit here is the adjective *naturalis*, as Sidney himself makes clear in his reference to "Empedocles, and Parmenides [who] sang their natural philosophy in verses" (*An Apology for Poetry*, ed. Forrest G. Robinson [Indianapolis: Bobbs-Merrill, 1970], 7–8). See below, Part II, for more on the "nameless" genres in antiquity and for George Puttenham's solution to the difficulty in giving this genre an English name; and n. 84.

Useful surveys of the Neo-Latin tradition in relation to classical antecedents are in James R. Naiden, *The Sphera of George Buchanan* (Philadelphia: n.p., 1952), Chap. 2, and Naiden, "Newton Demands the Latin Muse," *Symposium* 6 (May 1952), 111–20.

Students of the French tradition have long used the term "scientific poetry": Albert Marie Schmidt, *La Poésie Scientifique en France au Seizième Siècle* (Paris: Albin Michel, 1938); and Dudley Wilson, ed., *French Renaissance Scientific Poetry* (London: Athlone, 1974).

[10]This and the following paragraph are based largely on Baxter Hathaway, *The Age of Criticism: The Late Renaissance in Italy* (Ithaca: Cornell University Press, 1962), 20–22 and Chap. 4, "Were Empedocles and Lucretius Poets?" (65–80); see also Bernard Weinberg, *A History of Literary Criticism in the Italian Renaissance*, 2 vols. (Chicago: University of Chicago Press, 1961), passim and index, s.v. "scientific subjects."

There was, of course, an anti-scientific strain among certain humanists who elevated the "science of man" above the "science of nature"; for discussions of Petrarch, Bruni, Salutati, Piccolomini, Erasmus, Vives, and others in this light, see Eugenio Garin, *Italian Humanism: Philosophy and Civic Life in the Renaissance*, trans. Peter Muntz (Oxford: Blackwell, 1965), and Eugene F. Rice, Jr., *The Renaissance Idea of Wisdom* (Cambridge, Mass.: Harvard University Press, 1958).

Such extreme arguments were not unusual, nor was the prolif-
eration of positions in between those of the strict Aristotelians
and the "anti-Aristotelians." Paolo Beni, for example, tried to
show that Aristotle's mimesis was really the Platonic desideratum
of "simple narration," and on that basis he called Hesiod's *Works
and Days* and Virgil's *Georgics* "mimetic." G. P. Capriano insisted
on mimesis for true poetry but allowed that "natural things"
could be imitated "with fictions, adumbrating and veiling them
with the appearances and accidents of the senses [i.e., in myth]."
Thus he rejected Empedocles and Lucretius as genuine poets not
because they failed to imitate but because they did not write fictions, and he asserted that this is what Aristotle had said. Capriano, like Bacon's adversary Henry Reynolds (who thought
*Wisdom of the Ancients* was not strong enough in claiming the
ancient myths as repositories of scientific knowledge), approved
the Stoic conception of myth as embodying scientific truth.[11] Ludovico Castelvetro, who also believed his theory squared with
Aristotle, rejected Empedocles and others because they did not
invent anything new, invention (rather than imitation) being for
him the mark of a true poet. Going further, Castelvetro disal-
lowed any kind of instruction as an end in poetry, insisting its
sole purpose was to give pleasure. Thus, while he asserted that
Cicero, Quintilian, and Horace proved that they did not understand Aristotle when they called Empedocles a good poet, Castelvetro himself, claiming to follow Aristotle, ended up in the
extreme estheticism of ancient theorists like Callimachus, Eratos-
thenes, and Philodemus.[12] In this, Castelvetro was radically out
of tune with the pervasive didacticism of Renaissance poetic theory. His case is useful, though, in illustrating the degree to which
Aristotle could be interpreted to accommodate virtually any critical disposition. Generally speaking, however, scientific poetry
was a genre to be reckoned with; even those who considered
themselves strict Aristotelians could not "exclude completely

---

[11]This position is prominently exemplified in Crates of Mallos (fl. 160 B.C.) whose notion of geography, derived from an allegoresis of Homer in light of a Stoic physics, influenced cartography for a millennium and a half. See William H. Stahl, *Roman Science:
Origins, Development and Influence to the Later Middle Ages* (Madison: University of Wiscon-
sin Press, 1962), 60ff.; and A. M. Cinquemani, "Henry Reynolds' *Mythomystes* and the
Continuity of Ancient Modes of Allegoresis in Seventeenth-Century England," *PMLA* 85
(1970), 1041–49.

[12]In addition to Hathaway's remarks, see H. B. Charlton, *Castelvetro's Theory of Poetry*
(Manchester: Manchester University Press, 1913), 41–42, 66ff. The equation of poetry with
pleasure was always grist for the mills of those who attacked poetry as having no substantial purpose, from Plato to Bacon; see n. 31 below.

from the realms of poetry poets whose subject matter was abstract doctrine or speculation. Although not rejecting the limitation of poetic subject matter, they struggled valiantly to discover under what conditions the blanket proscription [against science] did not obtain."[13]

For most sixteenth-century English writers of poetic theory or criticism, scientific poetry posed no significant theoretical problem of the kind that troubled their Italian counterparts. The prevailing theory was the formalist, rhetorical one of the Middle Ages: any subject matter could be ornamented by versification. Hence, scientific verse was as unproblematical theoretically as scientific prose. When English humanists first turned their attention to the question of classical genres, they tended to classify poems as best they could, according to subject matter. This kind of primitive genre theory, along with a healthy Elizabethan chauvinism, could easily lead naive critics like Barnabe Googe, William Webbe, or Francis Meres to claim eagerly, for example, that Thomas Tusser's homely but extremely popular anapests on *A Hundreth Good Points of Husbandry* (1557; enlarged to *Five Hundred Points* by 1573 and reissued 13 more times by 1600) constituted a "georgic" poem and that Tusser was an English Hesiod or Virgil. Though he was no less concerned to elevate the status of English letters, the more sophisticated and philosophically-minded Sir Philip Sidney challenged both this kind of unrefined classicism and the older rhetorical conception of poetry. On the question of didactic-mimetic, his apparently strict Aristotelianism allies him with those Italian humanists who rejected scientific poetry, and the *Apology for Poetry* (composed ca. 1581–83, published 1595) seems to go out of its way to make a similar wholesale rejection of the "kind" of poetry that deals "with matters philosophical: either moral, as Tyrtaeus, Phocylides, and Cato; or natural, as Lucretius, and Virgil's *Georgics*; or astronomical, as Manilius and Pontanus; or historical, as Lucan . . . because this . . . sort is wrapped within the fold of the proposed subject, and takes not the course of his own invention"—even though he calls these poems "the sweet food of sweetly uttered knowledge."[14]

---

[13]Hathaway, *The Age of Criticism*, 80. See also Hathaway, *Marvels and Commonplaces: Renaissance Literary Criticism* (New York: Random House, 1968), 44–46, 92–94. Similar debates and opinions are to be found in sixteenth- and seventeenth-century France; see Schmidt, *Poésie Scientifique*, and Dwight L. Durling, *Georgic Tradition in English Poetry* (Morningside Heights, N.Y.: Columbia University Press, 1935), 6–16, who also surveys some of the English theories.

[14]*Apology*, 19–20; he further softens his rejection by adding, "whether they properly be poets or no let grammarians dispute."

This position, which lumps together poems on moral philosophy, science (with a confusing distinction between natural philosophy and astronomy), and history, and which ignores details like the mimetic elements in *De rerum natura* and the *Georgics*, Sidney is unable to sustain as his argument progresses. Such a statement was necessitated, however, by his overriding preoccupation with the ideal of a morally efficacious poetry which, he insists, can best achieve its peculiar impact mimetically (through representation) rather than didactically (through direct instruction). In fact, however, he repeatedly goes back on his theoretical exclusion of didactic poetry when his own argument requires him to underscore the value and venerability of poetry through the ages. In such contexts, he refers approvingly to scientific poetry, both ancient and modern. Sidney's apparent ambivalence toward scientific poetry can thus be traced to the polemical and defensive character of the *Apology*. Like Aristotle, Sidney falls victim to the rigidity of definitions that were invoked to meet a specific challenge to poetry. We cannot but agree with Elizabeth Sewell, who has cogently argued that in divorcing poetry from natural philosophy and other branches of knowledge, and yet at the same time asserting that poetry *is* philosophy and the source of true knowledge, Sidney is involved in a contradiction which is characteristic of "the muddle his century was in . . . about the connection between poetry and philosophy, myths and truth."[15] On the other hand, Sidney's ambivalence toward scientific poetry in particular was not shared by most Elizabethan critics, poets, or scientists. In fact, scientific poetry, both as a literary form and as a vehicle for scientific learning, was highly esteemed in all quarters.[16]

If, however, we turn to the figure whose views on scientific poetry would perhaps be of greatest value for understanding it in relation to the emergent cultural values of the early seventeenth century, we are liable, at least initially, to be disappointed. As the chief English voice of the new philosophy, as one who discusses

---

[15]*The Orphic Voice* (1960; rpt. New York: Harper, 1971), 73–74.

[16]For a full discussion of the material in the last two paragraphs, see Robert M. Schuler, "Theory and Criticism of the Scientific Poem in Elizabethan England," *English Literary Renaissance* 15 (1985), 3–41. By the Restoration, the status of scientific poetry was being debated even more actively. The culmination of this discussion was Joseph Addison's laudatory "Essay on the Georgics," appended to Dryden's 1697 translation of the works of Virgil, which spells out the theoretical basis for two of the most popular poetic forms of the next century: "georgic" (a term broadly applied to scientific, practical, and descriptive verse) and physico-theological poetry. See William Powell Jones, *The Rhetoric of Science* (Berkeley: University of California Press, 1966), and John Chalker, *The English Georgic: A Study in the Development of a Form* (London: Routledge & Kegan Paul, 1969).

the nature of poetry in relation to scientific learning, and as one whose pronouncements on rhetoric and style were to define the Royal Society's program for establishing the proper medium of scientific prose, Francis Bacon appears to have remarkably little to say about scientific poetry.

But ought we expect him to address the subject in the first place? From one point of view, no: Bacon was not primarily a literary theorist, and he must have thought most scientific poetry to be no better than most scientific prose—riddled with the errors stemming from the Four Idols. On the other hand, certain ancient scientific poems were fundamentally important to his own scientific philosophy. For while Bacon certainly condemned the traditional philosophies emanating either from Aristotle's system-building or from Plato's abstract intellectualism, he was significantly partial to "pre-Socratic naturalism and Democritean materialism"[17]—scientific theories preserved most fully, that is, in the chief Greek and Latin scientific poems of antiquity. Take, for example, the physics of Parmenides and Empedocles, which Bacon analyzes in several different works. These fifth-century Presocratics wrote their scientific poems at a time when prose had become the usual medium for both philosophy and science, and they are responsible for having established philosophical and scientific poetry as a genre.[18] As for the atomism of Leucippus and Democritus—the single most important scientific idea that Bacon found in antiquity—he found it most powerfully expounded in Lucretius' *De rerum natura*, a key text for him and (though rivaled by Virgil's *Georgics*) the single most important and influential scientific poem of antiquity.[19]

If these scientific poems were of such significance to Bacon, why then does he never, in his theoretical discussion of Poesy

---

[17]Paolo Rossi, *Francis Bacon: From Magic to Science*, trans. Sacha Rabinovitch (London: Routledge & Kegan Paul, 1968), 84.

[18]See Schuler and Fitch, "Theory and Context of the Didactic Poem," 4–5.

[19]Of course, Lucretius is looking back to Democritus from a post-Aristotelian vantage point in the context of Hellenistic syncretism; see Part IV below.

In various writings, Bacon lists the same classical authors who preserved the fragments of the Presocratics: Aristotle, Diogenes Laertius, Plutarch, Cicero, and Lucretius; see Benjamin Farrington, *The Philosophy of Francis Bacon* (Chicago: University of Chicago Press, 1964), 68, 84, 116. To these should be added Johannes Stobaeus, whose anthology of ancient texts, *Eclogae Physicae et Ethicae*, is an important source for the teachings of Empedocles probably used by Bacon; see *The Works of Francis Bacon*, ed. James Spedding, Robert L. Ellis, and Douglas D. Heath, 14 vols. (London: Longman, 1857–74; rpt. Stuttgart: Friedrich Frommann, 1963), III, 760, n. 1. Subsequent references to *Works* will be given parenthetically in the text.

and its genres, mention—much less examine—this kind of didactic poetry as a literary form? I suggest first that the argumentative strategy required by Bacon's program for the advancement of human learning simply could not accommodate comfortably a theoretical consideration of scientific poetry. But more than the mere *omission* of a kind of poetry that Bacon knew well and used widely, it is his deliberate *avoidance* of the subject that interests me here. For this avoidance signals the tensions and inconsistencies that cut across his various pronouncements on poetry, and it highlights the conflict between his literary theories and his own pragmatic appropriation of ancient scientific poetry. On the one hand, in his formal theorizing about the origin and nature of poetry, Bacon denies the name of Poesy to all non-mimetic verse (including scientific poetry); but on the other, he frequently cites these poems in his scientific and philosophical writings—a practice which both qualifies the impression that he devalued scientific poetry as such, and illustrates how deeply scientific poetry had penetrated his thinking.[20] An examination of Bacon's apparent ambivalence toward scientific poetry, my immediate interest, will show how, like Aristotle and Sidney before him, Bacon falls victim to his own *a priori* definition of poetry as mimesis. More importantly, though, it will illuminate a fundamental conflict in Bacon's thought at the root of such ambivalence: an unresolved tension between science and poetry, reason and the imagination.

---

[20]Bacon's theory and critical practice of mythic allegoresis, by which Parabolical Poesy (i.e., classical myth) becomes a source of both scientific ideas and scientific methodology, are also relevant here. While this subject as a whole is too large to be considered here, Bacon's use of scientific poetry in his exposition of certain myths will be touched on below (see also nn. 25, 33).

## II. EPISTEMOLOGY VS. POETICS IN BACON

What, first of all, are the philosophical and ideological bases of Bacon's theory of poetry, and why does he adopt the Aristotelian criterion of mimesis and thereby exclude the scientific poets from consideration? Whenever he engages a new topic in the *De dignitate et augmentis scientiarum* (1623), where we find his fullest theoretical account of poetry, Bacon is careful to classify and order its various divisions or parts. Book II sets out systematically to classify all knowledge, each branch of which he then takes up separately. Accordingly, in the first chapter, he divides "all Human Learning into History, Poesy, Philosophy; with reference to the three Intellectual Faculties,—Memory, Imagination, and Reason" (from the title of Book II, Chap. I; *Works*, IV, 292). Though not new, neither was this scheme of human knowledge universal; in fact, Bacon's choice of this particular hierarchical paradigm is a deliberate strategy, here at the very beginning of his overview of all learning, to allow him to identify science as the supreme discipline, aligned as it is with man's highest faculty.[21] Moreover, the first paragraph of this introductory chapter emphasizes that "Poesy" is to be narrowly understood as a manifestation of an inferior faculty of the soul, one that "feigns":

---

[21]According to J. E. Spingarn, ed., *Critical Essays of the Seventeenth Century*, 3 vols. (1957; rpt. Bloomington: Indiana University Press, 1963), I, 219, and J. W. H. Atkins, *English Literary Criticism: The Renascence*, 2nd ed. (London: Methuen, 1951), 264, Bacon's classification resembles that of Juan Huarte, whose *Examen de Ingenios* (1575) had been Englished by Richard Carew in 1594. John L. Harrison, "Bacon's View of Rhetoric, Poetry, and the Imagination," *Huntington Library Quarterly*, 20 (1957), 107-25, says that Bacon's classification was anticipated by "both Cardanus and Campanella" (109). A useful account of the whole subject is Karl R. Wallace, *Francis Bacon on the Nature of Man* (Urbana: University of Illinois Press, 1967).

Natural philosophy is superior to all other kinds of "Philosophy" or human knowledge because only this kind of knowledge was possessed by Adam before the Fall. Only after the loss of Paradise did man even have to invent moral or civil philosophy, the other two main branches in Bacon's scheme. On "Bacon's belief in a primeval bliss that philosophy must strive to recapture," see Rossi, 128-34, and Barbara Carman Garner, "Francis Bacon, Natalis Comes and the Mythological Tradition," *Journal of the Warburg and Courtauld Institutes* 33 (1970), 264-91, esp. 276-78, 288, 291.

The best division of human learning is that derived from the three faculties of the rational soul, which is the seat of learning. History has reference to the Memory, poesy to the Imagination, and philosophy to the Reason. And by poesy here I mean nothing else than feigned history or fables; for verse is but a character of style, and belongs to the arts of speech, whereof I will treat in its proper place.[22]

That last sentence is important, first in its identification of verse form as merely a matter of style. Even more significant, however, is Bacon's definition of Poesy as "feigned history or fables," a slight but crucial variation on Aristotle's "imitation of an action." This designation allows Bacon to situate both poetry and history—precisely because their mode is defined as essentially *narrative*, rather than discursive (the mode of philosophy or science)—in the lower compartments of his hierarchy. By reducing Poesy to narrative, he effectively excludes all discursive poetry, such as scientific poetry, from consideration. As Gerald F. Else points out, this is exactly what Aristotle himself had accomplished by juxtaposing Homer and Empedocles; for him, mimesis includes "*stories* about *men*," not "exposition, *argument* about elements, principles, or things" (*Aristotle's Poetics*, p. 53, n. 203).

The stylistic agitation of the passage just quoted is almost as revealing of Bacon's hierarchical thinking as its content. Note how the last sentence is given a special emphasis, by the way it abruptly returns to the second of the three pairs of mental functions and their products, and then proceeds to take over the rest of the paragraph. It is as if the unruly subject of Poesy has to be dealt with immediately, as if it cannot wait until Chapter XIII where its orderly turn is to come. The "And" with which the sentence begins also suggests Bacon's anxiety to contain the subject (and of course the disruptive effects of the Imagination itself) rather than waiting to "treat [it] in its proper place."

Such anxiety becomes understandable when we grasp the importance of this hierarchy of mental functions for Bacon's epistemology, upon which he bases humanity's claim to knowledge and truth. Throughout his philosophical writings, Bacon conceives of human knowledge as a pyramid, the base of which is "history" or "experience," with metaphysic at the penultimate

[22]*Works*, IV, 292. The "proper place" is later in *De augmentis*, under grammar and the arts of speech, Book VI, Chap. I (*Works*, IV, 438ff.). Bacon reiterates the distinction between verse form and poetic content there and in Book II, Chap. XIII, on Poesy (*Works*, IV, 314ff.), on which see below.

level. The vertical point is the "summary law of nature," which though it must be sought may finally be beyond man's capacity.[23] Bacon's inductive epistemology parallels this ascending pattern, the mind dealing first with "individuals" and only later with "abstract notions." The hierarchy of all human learning set out in the introductory chapter of Book II of the *De augmentis* obviously follows this inductive model; it carefully reserves the mind's highest functions—that is, any sort of abstract discourse—for Reason and Philosophy (science), and it firmly places both Memory and the Imagination (and thus History and Poesy) at the base of the pyramid of knowledge. This point is made explicit in the opening sentences of each of the next three paragraphs: "History is properly concerned with individuals, which are circumscribed by place and time. . . . Poesy, *in the sense in which I have defined the word*, is also concerned with individuals . . . [But] Philosophy discards individuals . . ." (*Works*, IV, 292; emphasis added). The underscored qualification indicates the deliberateness of Bacon's reductive definition of Poesy, as well as a slight self-consciousness about it, but the following paragraph is wholly devoted to justifying his distinction between Poesy and History, on the one hand, and Philosophy on the other. That such a division is correct, Bacon says,

may be easily seen by observing the commencements of the intellectual process. The sense, which is the door of the intellect, is affected by individuals only. The images of those individuals—that is, the impressions which they make on the sense—fix themselves in the memory, and pass into it in the first instance entire as it were, just as they come. These the human mind proceeds to review and ruminate; and thereupon either simply rehearses them, or makes fanciful imitations of them, or analyses and classifies them. Wherefore from these three fountains, Memory, Imagination, and Reason, flow these three emanations, History, Poesy, and Philosophy; and there can be no others. For I consider history and experience to be the same thing, as also philosophy and the sciences.[24]

---

[23]This central theory is repeatedly expressed; see, e.g., *New Atlantis* (*Works*, III, 164–65), *Advancement* (III, 356), *Novum Organum*, I, aphorism XIX (IV, 50), and *De augmentis* (IV, 321–22, 361). For a detailed discussion of this theory and the specific faculty psychology underlying it, see Lisa Jardine, *Francis Bacon: Discovery and the Art of Discourse* (Cambridge: Cambridge University Press, 1974), Chap. 4 (esp. 88–108) and Chap. 6.

[24]*Works*, IV, 292–93; a parallel passage in *Descriptio globi intellectualis* defines Philosophy further: "For under philosophy I include all arts and sciences, and in a word whatever has been from the occurrence of individual objects collected and digested by the mind into general notions" (*Works*, V, 504).

Hence the role of Poesy and the Imagination is further reduced to that of making "fanciful imitations" of individual sense experiences. In this context, where Bacon is establishing the pecking order necessary for his elevation of the scientific enterprise, mimesis is clearly not a very significant undertaking.

When he considers more fully the nature of Poesy in the chapter assigned to it (XIII), however, Bacon allows rather more to the Imagination, and the rigidity of his original categories begins to break down. Take, for example, his account of Narrative Poesy, the form closest to History. We learn, first, that such mimetic poetry actually ranks above factual history. Narrative Poesy is superior to history because it can create events "of sufficient grandeur to satisfy the human mind" and can modify the outcome of events "according to merit and the law of providence"; further, instead of wearying the mind with "satiety of ordinary events" as "true history" does, "Poesy refreshes it, by reciting things unexpected and various and full of vicissitudes. So that this Poesy conduces not only to delight but also to magnanimity and morality" (Works, IV, 316).

This is a common enough claim in Renaissance literary theory, but it is difficult to see how it can be reconciled with Bacon's earlier claim that Poesy, like History, is limited to representing only the concrete particulars of "experience." How, one must ask, can poetry lead to "magnanimity and morality" without the "human mind" operating in exactly the same way it does in relation to philosophy or science? That is, to arrive at moral principles, must it not move "upward" from mere "sense" (here, the particular details of a "feigned history" or narrative) through a process of abstraction, just as the Reason acts upon experience ("For I consider history and experience to be the same thing") to arrive at general scientific or philosophical axioms? Moreover, is it not the poet's imagination that embodies the abstract in the concrete?[25] While Bacon cannot in this context stress the point, he is

---

[25]This problem becomes even more acute in relation to Bacon's subsequent discussion of Parabolical Poesy; for the primary importance of scientifically interpreted myths in Bacon's mythography (i.e., Parabolical Poesy), see Garner, "Francis Bacon, Natalis Comes and the Mythological Tradition," and Jardine, 192. See also n. 33, below.

That Bacon attributes to the Imagination the power to move from specific details to general notions is clear from his criticism elsewhere of the Imagination in too hastily creating systems of thought from a few particular instances; see, e.g., Works, IV, 56; V, 503–504. Jardine points out other inconsistencies in Bacon's faculty psychology and the resulting classification of knowledge according to Memory, Imagination, and Reason, showing, e.g., that in the discussion of civil history even the Memory is capable of generalization and interpretation. This classification "does, however, provide a particularly good setting for *philosophy*" and allows Bacon to avoid the traditional split of knowledge into theoretical and practical (*Francis Bacon: Discovery and the Art of Discourse*, 97–98). The overriding desire to valorize philosophy and science is again apparent.

in fact going beyond Aristotle's famous assertion that "poetry is a more philosophical and a higher thing than history: for poetry tends to express the universal, history the particular," in that Bacon's "universals" (magnanimity and morality) are at a higher level of abstraction than Aristotle's ("how a person of a certain type will on occasion speak or act . . ."). He is also, it would seem, dangerously close to endorsing Sidney's further claim that poetry surpasses *both* history and philosophy—because only the "peerless poet . . . coupleth the general notion with the particular example"—a claim that would actually displace philosophy from its pre-eminent position at the top of Bacon's epistemological hierarchy.[26] Bacon escapes confronting this dilemma by stressing two aspects of Poesy that are presented as particularly non-rational: its *origins* in the Imagination, and the emotive *responses* it engenders in its readers. This strategy ends, however, in contradiction.

He goes on, first, vaguely to suggest that because of its moral efficacy Narrative Poesy "may be fairly thought to partake somewhat of a divine nature" (*Works*, IV, 316); he thereby associates it with a realm of "knowledge" beyond human reason and therefore conveniently outside his own discourse, since (as he repeatedly warns) one should not "unwisely mingle or confound" human knowledge and religion.[27] Poesy's "divine" character does not, however, *elevate* it in relation to the human learning of science, even though "it raises the mind and carries it aloft"; rather, this metaphor evokes the modern sense of "flightiness," and the seductive "charms" of Poesy, along with the "sweet access" provided by its "music" (which may refer either to primitive poetry, which was sung, or to meter generally), add to the impression that Poesy is fanciful, insubstantial, and ultimately suspect.

These interrelated points are made explicit in a discussion of the Imagination later in the *De augmentis*, as a brief look at Book V, Chap. I, will show. This chapter identifies the two kinds of

---

[26]*Apology*, 27. Sidney, of course, has *moral* philosophy specifically in mind, while Bacon is speaking more generally of the rational faculty capable of abstraction. See also, however, Sidney's assertion that "the skill of the artificer standeth in that *Idea* or fore-conceit of the work, and not in the work itself" (16).

Earlier in the same paragraph on Narrative Poesy just cited, Bacon actually comes close to Sidney's "golden world" idea: "For if the matter be attentively considered, a sound argument may be drawn from Poesy, to show that there is agreeable to the spirit of man a more ample greatness, a more perfect order, and a more beautiful variety than it can anywhere (since the Fall) find in nature" (IV, 315-16). Some similarities between Sidney and Bacon regarding poetry's moral value are discussed by Harrison, "Bacon's View of Rhetoric," 112-13.

[27]*Advancement*, *Works*, III, 268; see also *Novum Organum*, Book I, aphorism LXV (*Works*, IV, 65-66).

knowledge relating to the human soul: Logic (which "discourses of the Understanding and Reason . . . [and] produces determinations"), and Ethic (which "discourses . . . of the Will, Appetite, and Affections . . . [and] produces actions") (*Works*, IV, 405). We are at the nexus between thought and action, *gnosis* and *praxis*. Here Bacon explains that the Imagination acts as a "messenger or proctor" to both the Reason and the Will, in which capacity it is a "Janus," with "two different faces, for the face towards reason has the print of truth, and the face towards action has the print of goodness." But the Imagination is also capable of taking control of both Reason and Will. First in a good way: "For we see that in matters of faith and religion our imagination raises itself above our reason; not that divine illumination resides in the imagination; its seat being rather in the very citadel of the mind and understanding; but that the divine grace uses the motions of the imagination as an instrument of illumination, . . . which is the reason why religion ever sought access to the mind by similitudes, types, parables, visions, dreams." He immediately adds, however, that Imagination can also gain an undesirable eminence:

And again it is no small dominion which imagination holds in persuasions that are wrought by eloquence; for when by arts of speech men's minds are soothed, inflamed, and carried hither and thither, it is all done by stimulating the imagination till it becomes ungovernable, and not only sets reason at nought, but offers violence to it, partly by blinding, partly by incensing it. Nevertheless, I see no cause to alter the former division [i.e., between the rational and moral faculties of the soul]; for imagination hardly produces sciences; poesy (which in the beginning was referred to imagination) being to be accounted rather as a pleasure or play of wit than a science. And for the power of the imagination in nature, I have just now assigned it to the doctrine concerning the soul. And its relation to rhetoric I think best to refer to that art itself, which I shall handle hereafter [i.e., Book VI, Chap. III].[28]

---

[28]*Works*, IV, 406. Jerry Weinberger's lengthy commentary on the corresponding passage in *Advancement* points out some of the contradictions in Bacon's various pronouncements on the Imagination; this remark is indicative of what he finds: "As judged by reason's virtue, the imagination is the locus of error, but even so, the imagination's power actually to make what it will can have its own independent charm. Of course the poetic art depends upon such charm, so it is no wonder that Bacon says there is no science of the imagination. And this lack does not conflict with the imagination's having some work: the imagination's work is its service to science or reason" (*Science, Faith, and Politics: Francis Bacon and the Utopian Roots of the Modern Age* [Ithaca: Cornell University Press, 1985], 265; see also 266–68).

The abrupt shifts here—from the positive to the negative sides of the Imagination (it is "an instrument of illumination" but it "offers violence to [reason]"), and then from the inflammatory "arts of speech" to ludic "poesy"—bespeak both the contradictions within Bacon's conception of the Imagination itself, which has both a divine and a demonic side, and his anxiety to contain and demean this undeniably powerful "Janus," whose faces no longer bear merely the "print" of "truth" and "goodness."

John M. Cocking has pointed out that similar contradictions operate in the *Novum Organum*, where Bacon's theory of "forms" depends on a uniform correspondence between sensible qualities (particulars) and fundamental states of matter (abstract principles). At times, Bacon both accepts and denies the certainty of the senses, but in the end he must rescue his inductive theory by reasserting the validity of "thinking . . . by means of images provided by the senses. And this brings Bacon back to a formulation very like Aristotle's; imagination . . . is the messenger running to and fro between the sensible world and the human reason." But while this much was necessary for his new induction, Bacon stops short of accepting the full power of the imagination that Aristotle had given it:

> Although Bacon maintained the "messenger" function of imagination as set out by Aristotle, he deprived imagination of what Aristotle called its "deliberative" or "calculative" function of "separating" and "combining" images. Separating and combining, said Bacon, can properly be carried out by reason alone.

Yet he implied in many contexts that the free ranging of the mind encouraged by imagination may, as it were by luck rather than judgement, hit upon some useful or even true belief. There are three sciences, wrote Bacon, "which have had better intelligence and confederacy with the imagination of man than with his reason"; they are "Astrology, Natural Magic and Alchemy." These are "full of error and vanity," but noble in their aims and sometimes effective through their blind and unreasoning gropings and their accidental findings [*Works*, III, 289]. . . . Since humanity had not had the benefit of scientific induction before Bacon but had nevertheless achieved some practically useful knowledge, reason and imagination working haphazardly must have had some effect. But Bacon will hardly allow even this ranging of the mind, this accidental hitting upon some truth, to imagination. Consistently the "image" as the mind's contact with reality is good; "imagination" as a process of thought is bad. And almost consistently, . . . Bacon uses *imaginatio* and its associated words for "good" imagination and *phantasia* and its derivatives for its vicious use in thinking, or its comparatively trivial use in poetry.[29]

It should be no surprise that the Latin versions of all the passages cited in the present discussion employ the term *phantasia*. This linguistic ploy, lost in translation, is perhaps indicative of the inadequacy of language either to conceal fully or to clarify Bacon's ambivalence or self-contradiction with regard to the Imagination.

We can now return to Book II, Chap. XIII, where Bacon has just claimed that Narrative Poesy "conduces not only to delight but also to magnanimity and morality." With his views on the Imagination (*phantasia*) in mind, we can appreciate more fully the backhandedness of the compliment he now extends to Narrative Poesy:

Whence it may be fairly thought to partake somewhat of a divine nature; because it raises the mind and carries it aloft, accommodating the shows of things to the desires of the mind, not (like reason and history) buckling and bowing down the mind to the nature of things. And by these charms, and that agreeable congruity which it has with man's nature, accompanied also with music, to gain more sweet access, it has so won its way as to have been held in honor even in the rudest ages and among barbarous peoples, when other kinds of learning were utterly excluded.[30]

Instead of allowing mimetic Poesy to do what he has just claimed it can—to ascend from specific narrative details to the abstract principles of "magnanimity and morality"—Bacon characterizes Poesy's "ascent" as a kind of unrestrained wish-fulfillment or

---

[29]"Bacon's View of Imagination," *Francis Bacon: Terminologia e Fortuna nel XVII Secolo,* Lessico Intellettuale Europeo XXXIII, ed. Marta Fattori (Rome: Edizioni dell'Ateneo, 1984), 43–58; quotations are from pp. 52, 52–53. See also Marta Fattori, "*Phantasia* nella classificazione baconiana della scienze," in the same collection, 117–37.

[30]*Works,* IV, 316. Here is Jerry Weinberger's comment on the corresponding passage in the *Advancement:* "Bacon says that poetry serves magnanimity, morality, and delectation but only by submitting the appearances of things to the 'desires of the mind' and that in this respect it differs from reason, which submits the mind to the nature of things. But in the *Novum organum,* Bacon says that reason bows to nature in order to conquer her. Moreover, in discussing the history of the arts, Bacon noted that, when nature is vexed by art, she is likened to Proteus, who, when 'straitened and held fast,' would change his shape. What Bacon here calls the feigned liberty of poetry is actually promised by the scientific mastery of nature, and so the liberty of poetry is actually to be found in the new method for discovering all things" (*Science, Faith, and Politics,* 241).

pandering to "the desires of the mind."[31] In doing so, he both undercuts his generous attribution of a "divine nature" to Poesy and tries to dissociate the kind of "ascent" of which Poesy is capable from the ascending method of knowledge by which Reason alone can arrive at first principles.[32] The same concern can be seen in the passage cited earlier, where he hastily adds, "for imagination hardly produces sciences." This statement in turn recalls the ambiguous account of astrology, natural magic, and alchemy (contradictorily, they are "sciences" produced through "a confederacy with the imagination"), where the Imagination does and does not lead to abstract truth by way of particulars. In one context Imagination is a means to "magnanimity and morality" (and thus presumably to knowledge and truth), while in another it can yield only "error and vanity."

A similar confusion is apparent in Bacon's description of the reader's rather irrational *response* to poetry—as he or she is diverted, "carried away," or merely "refreshed" by the "charms" of Poesy's "acts and events." That is, while Bacon, like most Renaissance literary theorists, clearly *assumes* the moral intentionality of the mimetic poet (and the positive affective response to be gained from representations of "morality and magnanimity"), he dares not pursue the implications of that assumption (as Sidney had), lest Poesy usurp the throne of knowledge reserved for science alone. What Bacon obviously cannot countenance is the thought—against which we repeatedly see him struggling—that science and poetry might actually operate in analogous ways, that Reason and Imagination are not opposite and mutually exclusive poles of the human mind.

Bacon's anxiety to preserve the distinctions between Reason and Imagination and to restrict Poesy to the act of "fanciful imitation" is, in fact, apparent from the very beginning of Chapter XIII, when he first formally addresses the subject of Poesy and classifies it. By stressing the division between form and content,

---

[31]The negative thrust of "accommodating" here is intensified not only by the contrasting masculine force of Reason's "buckling and bowing," but also by the association of the "charms" of music with "the rudest ages and . . . barbarous peoples." The whole passage is reminiscent of Plato's critique of music in *Republic*, Book III, where the irrationality of rhythm, melody, and dance is analyzed. Behind such a distrust of poetry is the old notion (found in the sophist Gorgias, ca. 483–376 B.C.) that poets compose to give pleasure, not to convey truth; compare Castelvetro, above, and see Schuler and Fitch, "Theory and Context of the Didactic Poem," 7–8.

[32]For the centrality of Bacon's "ascending" and "descending" methods, see Jardine, 34, 98–100.

he stresses both the laxity of the Imagination and the particularity of Poesy:

I now come to Poesy, which is a part of learning in measure of words for the most part restrained, but in all other points extremely free and licensed; and therefore (as I said at first) it is referred to the Imagination, which may at pleasure make unlawful matches and divorces of things. Now Poesy (as I have already observed) is taken in two senses; in respect of words or matter. In the first sense it is but a character of speech; for verse is only a kind of style and a certain form of elocution, and has nothing to do with the matter; for both true history may be written in verse and feigned history in prose. But in the latter sense, I have set it down from the first as one of the principal branches of learning, and placed it by the side of history; being indeed nothing else but an imitation of history at pleasure. (*Works*, IV, 314–15)

Having delimited Poesy to "history at pleasure," Bacon can now logically proceed to his classification of poetic kinds, which deliberately excludes all those genres that do not adhere strictly to the central criterion of mimetic action. His discussion is thus limited to Narrative, Dramatic, and Parabolical Poesy. Again, his motive springs not from a conviction that the mimetic is a morally or esthetically superior form of art, but from a desire to remove from the category of Poesy any kind of discursive or reflective writing— however traditional—that could claim to be the product of Reason, rather than of the Imagination. Hence he arbitrarily refuses to follow "custom and the divisions which are received"; he will dismiss "from the present discourse Satires, Elegies, Epigrams, Odes, and the like; and refer them to philosophy and arts of speech. And under the name of Poesy . . . treat only of feigned history."[33]

By "refer[ring] them to *philosophy*," though, Bacon implicitly acknowledges that some traditional non-mimetic poetic genres are indeed products of Reason. Among them would have to stand the scientific poems of Empedocles, Parmenides, Lucretius, and others. Not only, however, does Bacon fail to state this explic-

---

[33]*Works*, IV, 315. The extent to which Parabolical Poesy can be considered "feigned history" in the same sense as Narrative and Dramatic is dubious. Bacon's initial definition of Parabolical Poesy is "typical History, by which *ideas* that are objects of the *intellect* are represented in *forms* that are objects of the *sense*" (IV, 315; emphasis added). Even within the categories so carefully constructed to exclude discursive poetry, we can see a violation of the idea that Imagination/Poesy deals only with "individuals," and Reason/Philosophy with "abstract notions." In fact, with regard to Parabolical Poesy, Bacon clearly accepts the Sidneyan *Idea or fore-conceit* that animates the whole work.

itly, but the only division of "philosophy" under which he considers the non-mimetic genres is the "arts of speech," in *De augmentis,* Book VI, Chap. I. A brief look at this collateral chapter will show again how Bacon's categories collapse under the strain of his own argument.

In Book II, Chap. XIII, Bacon distinguishes clearly between the *essential* mimetic subject matter of poetry and its *incidental* external form ("for both true history may be written in verse and feigned history in prose"). In Book VI, Chap. I, he initially tries to maintain this divorce of form and content, but in the next breath asserts that matter and form ought to be inseparable:

> The Measure of words has produced a vast body of art; namely Poesy, considered with reference not to the matter of it (of which I have spoken above), but to the style and form of words: that is to say, meter or verse; wherein the art [i.e., theory] we have is a very small thing, but the examples are large and innumerable. Neither should that art (which the grammarians call Prosody) be confined to the teaching of the kinds and measures of verse. *Precepts should be added as to the kinds of verse which best suit each matter or subject.* The ancients used hexameter for histories [i.e., epics] and eulogies [and, as Bacon obviously knew, for didactic poems]; elegiac for complaints; iambic for invectives; lyric for odes and hymns. Nor have modern poets been wanting in this wisdom, so far as their own languages are concerned. (*Works,* IV, 443; emphasis added)

It appears that because he is not at the moment addressing the desideratum of mimetic subject matter for poetry, Bacon can speak of poetry as most writers on the subject do: as though it had many subjects, genres (mimetic and non-mimetic), and verse forms. But when, as in Book II, Chap. XIII, the thrust of his primary argument requires "feigned history" to be the only proper subject matter of poetry—so as to be congruent with his epistemology and hierarchy of knowledge—he must say that only mimetic works (whether Narrative, Dramatic, or Parabolical) are genuine Poesy.

That he uses the same term, "Poesy," in one context "with reference . . . to the matter of it" while in another "with reference . . . to the style and form of words," can be seen as a testimony to the awkwardness of literary terminology and as a momentary concession to the usual association of poetry with versification. Just as telling, though, is the inadvertent inclusion here of "histories," or epics, in a discussion that was intended—so he says, at least, in Chap. XIII of Book II—to deal only with

the traditional *non-mimetic* poetic genres, which he "refer[s] . . .
to philosophy and the arts of speech." In other words, while Bacon can assert earlier that "both true history may be written in
verse and feigned history [epic] in prose," the "ancients" to
whom he refers here did not in fact write epics in prose. Back in
Book II, Chap. XIII, Bacon had tried to anticipate this problem
when addressing "Narrative Poesy,—or Heroical, if you like so to
call it (understanding it of the matter, not of the verse)" (*Works,*
IV, 315). There he is speaking of the "Heroical" subject matter of
mimetic narrative (whether in verse or prose) as one of the three
branches of Poesy—Narrative, Dramatic, and Parabolical. But as
the lengthy passage quoted from Book VI, Chap. I shows, such
subject matter was always, in classical times, written in hexameters. In this context, Bacon's use of the word *histories,* rather than
*heroics* or *epics,* is thus a disingenuous (and unsuccessful) effort to
dissociate the matter and form of classical epic.

Similarly, the other genres included in Bacon's discussion of
meter—that is, the non-mimetic genres previously excluded from
the category of Poesy—are all *poetic* genres: that is, like epic itself,
they were executed only in verse, a fact indicated by the ancient
association of specific meters with certain subjects, as Bacon himself says. The facts of literary history, awkwardly for Bacon, pro-
claim a fusion of form and content, despite his earlier efforts to
deny their connection.

Particularly interesting here is Bacon's failure to acknowledge
didactic or scientific poetry as one of the major genres (along
with epic and eulogy) for which the ancients reserved the digni-
fied hexameter. In antiquity, didactic poetry was virtually never
distinguished from epic, all lengthy hexameter poems in the high
style being described by the Greeks as *epê* (plural of *epos,* "epic
poem").[34] Whether or not Bacon was aware of this point of terminology, he deliberately uses the term *histories* instead of *epics* or
*heroics* and thus narrows, rather than widens, the category to
which he refers. That he also names eulogies (a much less significant genre than the didactic poem) also suggests that his exclusion, or rather avoidance, of didactic is deliberate. But why?

---

[34]Butcher's translation of the sentence preceding Aristotle's rejection of Empedocles tries
to make this clear by adding a crucial parenthesis: "People . . . speak of elegiac poets, or
epic (that is, hexameter) poets . . ." (9). For the use of hexameters in classical didactic, see
W. S. Maguinness, "The Language of Lucretius," in *Lucretius,* ed. D. R. Dudley (London:
Routledge & Kegan Paul, 1965), 69–93, esp. 82–83; and Schuler and Fitch, "Theory and
Context of the Didactic Poem," p. 3 and nn. 11, 12, 13.

By now it should be clear that Bacon had his own reasons for not confronting directly the thorny problem that scientific poetry posed for the continental humanist critics and poets mentioned above. The literary humanists were concerned lest the highly esteemed poems of Hesiod, Lucretius, or Virgil (in the *Georgics*) should come under Aristotle's proscription of Empedocles. Bacon, on the contrary, was concerned that such texts—especially the discursive, theoretical, scientific ones like *De rerum natura*—would be considered as Poesy at all: not because their greatness urged that they be accepted into the canon, but because Poesy would thereby enter the domain of natural philosophy. His strategy is thus simply to eschew the subject of scientific poetry, even when his avowed topic is the nature and forms of poetry, and even when it would be most logical to include it. Given his own extensive appropriation of scientific poetry, such an absence is odd, to say the least. But given his epistemology and the need to preserve at all costs the correlative hierarchy of Reason (Philosophy) over Memory (History) and Imagination (Poesy), we can certainly understand it.

A further appreciation of Bacon's reluctance to engage the subject is gained by returning briefly to the issue of the relationship between verse form and subject matter. That I have not overstated the case for Bacon's anxiety over the question of scientific poetry is clear, I think, from the solution offered to the problem of generic names and poetic meter by a lesser writer who is (in this matter, at least) more disinterested than Bacon can be. George Puttenham's *Arte of English Poetry* (1589), like Bacon's discussion in *De augmentis* Book VI, identifies the various classical genres by the verse form they employ, each poet taking "a surname, as to be called a Poet Heroick, Lyrick, Elegiack, Epigrammatist, or otherwise."[35] Because "Heroick" meter had been pre-empted, as it were, by the writers of epic, Puttenham can find no similar "surname" for composers of didactic poetry; he does not, however, allow this semantic difficulty to deter him. Instead, he unpretentiously makes up his own descriptive term and proceeds to devote an entire chapter to the genre he calls simply, "The forme wherein honest and profitable artes and sciences were treated." However inelegant his name for didactic poetry may be, Puttenham is at least honest enough to deal with a

[35]In G. Gregory Smith, ed., *Elizabethan Critical Essays*, 2 vols. (Oxford: Clarendon Press, 1904), II, 26.

topic that does not fit into a pre-determined syntactic schema ("A Poet Heroick, Lyrick, Epigrammatist, . . ."). Furthermore, he deals directly with the facts and implications of the hexameter as the customary verse form of didactic poetry. The practical and scientific subjects of this genre, he says,

> were treated by Poets in verse *Exameter* sauouring the *Heroical,* and for the grauitie and comelinesse of the meetre most vsed with the Greekes and Latines to sad purposes. Such were the Philosophicall works of *Lucretius Carus* among the Romaines, the Astronomicall of *Aratus* and *Manilius,* one Greeke, th'other Latine, the Medicinall of *Nicander,* and that of *Oppianus* of hunting and fishes, and many moe that were too long to recite in this place.[36]

Like most Elizabethan theorists, Puttenham is able to acknowledge the didactic poets' use of the hexameter as appropriate to "sad" or serious purposes, and to name without embarrassment some of the chief practitioners. By contrast, Bacon's doctrine of mimesis (which we can now see as a calculated means of reducing Poesy to "feigned history" which supposedly deals only with "particulars") will not even allow a direct discussion of this discursive genre.

Thus in his poetic theory Bacon deliberately, but only with some difficulty, avoids facing the esthetic and philosophical implications of a mimetic poetry that is able to embody moral abstractions in its narrative particulars. More germane here, but for similar reasons, he eschews the epistemological implications of a didactic scientific poetry that was as capable of observation, analysis, and abstraction as was scientific prose. At stake in both instances are his hierarchical and supposedly discrete categories of Memory, Imagination, and Reason. But just as these categories do in fact break down even within Bacon's theoretical elaboration of them, so ancient scientific poetry finds its way into the very heart of his scientific philosophy.

---

[36]Smith, II, 46. D. W. Lucas notes how in *Poetics* 47b9–24 Aristotle's "explanation of the 'nameless' forms leads on to a digression on the naming of forms in terms of metre, a practice which conceals the difference between mimetic and non-mimetic writing"; see his edition of the Greek text of *Poetics* (Oxford: Clarendon, 1968), commentary p. 59. This confusion, like that over the mimetic-didactic question, was obviously another Renaissance inheritance from the *Poetics.*

## III. BACON AND THE PRESOCRATIC POET-PHILOSOPHERS

Writers of Renaissance scientific prose frequently cite ancient and modern scientific poems. Such allusions can, of course, be merely illustrative or even decorative, manifesting the author's learning, copiousness, or stylistic nicety. Not infrequently, however, one finds verse passages cheek-by-jowl with technical prose, serving the same discursive or instructional function: Virgil's *Georgics* cited in a practical handbook on agriculture or horsebreeding; passages from Oppian translated in an early Elizabethan book on popular natural history or (over 130 years later) in *The Philosophical Transactions of the Royal Society*; a snippet from Giovanni Pontano's long poem *Meteorum liber* translated in a Jacobean astronomical treatise; or Lucretius excerpted in a popular *Geography*.[37] Of Bacon's numerous allusions to the classical scientific poets, some are illustrative and non-scientific in purpose,[38] and he is noticeably sparing in

---

[37]For Hesiod's *Works and Days* and Virgil's *Georgics* treated as practical treatises on farming, see Schuler, "Theory and Criticism of the Scientific Poem," 29–32 and Leonard Mascall, *The Countryman's Jewel: or the Government of Cattel* (1680); for Oppian, John Maplet, *A Greene Forest, or a Natural History* (1567; this work also contains passages from the *Georgics*) and *Philosophical Transactions*, vol. 20, no. 239, pp. 105–64 (April 1698; separately printed, STC T3597); for Pontano, Fredericus Nausea, *A Treatise of Blazing Starres in General*, trans. Abraham Fleming (1618); for Lucretius, Nathaniel Carpenter, *Geography* (1625).

[38]These will not be considered here. For various "literary" uses of the *Georgics*, see, e.g., *De augmentis*, *Works*, IV, 285, 287, 362, 409–10; *Redargutio Philosophorum*, *Works*, III, 577 (trans. Farrington, *The Philosophy of Francis Bacon*, 124). For Virgilian material applied to moral or political philosophy in at least four myths in *Wisdom of the Ancients*, see Charles W. Lemmi, *The Classical Deities in Bacon: A Study in Mythological Symbolism* (1933; rpt. Folcroft, Pennsylvania: Folcroft Press, 1969), 73, 119, 176, 186, 189. For Virgilian quotations dealing with these subjects in the *Advancement*, see Weinberger, *Science, Faith, and Politics*, index, s.v. Virgil; and for the *Georgics* as used in these non-scientific contexts, see esp. pp. 156, 160, 231, 248, 307.

Lucretian passages or allusions can serve philosophical ends in the *Essays*; see D. S. Brewer, "Lucretius and Bacon on Death," *Notes & Queries*, 200 (1955), 509–10; and *Works*, IV, 466–67. Or they can be rhetorical and illustrative, as in *The Advancement* (*Works*, III, 317–18) or *Novum Organum* (IV, 114); in both these cases, Bacon adopts striking Lucretian metaphors with which to conclude the first major division of each work. For the influence of Lucretian moral and political ideas in *Wisdom*, see Howard B. White, *Antiquity Forgot: Essays on Shakespeare, Bacon, and Rembrandt* (The Hague: Martinus Nijhoff, 1978), 125–26, 129–31. For a gnomic saying from Hesiod on the importance of timeliness, see *Works*, IV, 466.

his quotations from modern poets of science.[39] However, most of his references to the ancient scientific poets are made for their scientific import—not in the servile manner of contemporary popularizers of science who saw them as unquestionably trustworthy authorities, but in the manner of one who scrutinized all of ancient science for whatever value it might have for the instauration of learning. By examining his various appropriations of the Presocratic poet-philosophers, of Lucretius, and of Virgil, we can correct the impression, given by his theoretical statements on Poesy, that Bacon neither knew nor valued this kind of poetry. Moreover, we will see, especially in his deployment of Virgilian excerpts, that he fails to maintain the categorical distinctions between Reason and Imagination, science and poetry, that are so important to his epistemology and the theoretical foundations of his scientific program.

Even though he always remained faithful to his conviction that "science is to be sought from the light of nature, not from the darkness of antiquity," Bacon had a special admiration for the Presocratic philosophers. Farrington has shown how, during the formative years of 1607–1608, Bacon developed an appreciation of their achievement, as well as a more discriminating perception of "antiquity":

He sensed in their fragments a more direct contact with nature than in later Greek schools and, in his enthusiasm, made a pioneer study of their scattered remains which was to be of importance for the scholarship of the nineteenth century. He developed a preference for the materialism of Democritus over the idealism of Plato; and his sense of the superiority of the natural philosophy of Empedocles and Democritus over the logic and metaphysics of Aristotle and Plato became the chief example, if not the very foundation, of his view that the river of time bears down to us on its surface the slighter and emptier relics of the past and drowns the more solid achievements in its depths.[40]

---

[39]I have found only one reference to the extremely popular Du Bartas (*Advancement, Works*, III, 281), but this is on an ethical point. Bacon does cite an obscure Latin alchemical poem by Johannes Pratensis (*Historia ventorum*, V, 154) and some unattributed Latin lines on astrology (*De augmentis*, IV, 355); see n. 89, below.

[40]*The Philosophy of Francis Bacon*, 48; cf. *Novum Organum*, I, LXXI; *Works*, IV, 72. Farrington points out (48–50) that during this same period Bacon developed an intense interest in the hidden meaning of ancient myths which eventuated in *Wisdom of the Ancients*. In his overall scheme of history, the Presocratics are the first scientists actually known. They were preceded by the ancient, unknown sages who, sometime after the Fall, recovered a good deal of Adam's lost mastery over nature and inscribed their knowledge in "fables" or myths which were then passed down through time by the poets. The latter sometimes

Certainly the most important of the Presocratics for Bacon was Democritus, and we will see later how Bacon habitually found his atomic physics in the scientific poem of Lucretius. Of the six other Presocratic philosophers cited most frequently in Bacon's scientific works, however, three—Xenophanes, Parmenides, and Empedocles—wrote in verse,[41] though Bacon never refers to them as poets and usually paraphrases rather than quotes directly.[42]

Of these poet-philosophers, Xenophanes (ca. 570-475 B.C.) is both the earliest and the least well preserved. Although he is credited with a poem *On Nature*, he probably did not write a formal work on physical matters, and Bacon makes relatively little use of him. He is, however, listed twice among the Presocratics deserving more study (*Works*, IV, 358; Farrington, p. 84), and in the *Historia vitae et mortis* Bacon characterizes his philosophical concerns—"the survey of the universe, the variety of nature, unbounded, deep and noble thoughts concerning the infinite, the stars, the heroic virtues"—as being conducive to longevity. Here he is tellingly grouped with Democritus and Philolaus of Croton, and his thought contrasted with the "crabbed and narrow" principles of the "peripatetics and schoolmen," whose contentious wrangling leads to an early death (*Works*, V, 263). In the same work (V, 246) and in the *Redargutio philosophorum* Bacon alludes to the humorous anecdote that because of the diversity of his opinions his name was changed "from Xenophanes (Revealer of new things) to Xenomanes (Mad about novelties)." In the latter context, this story is held up as a warning to William Gilbert, whose "affection for Xenophanes ought to

---

embellished the basic stories of the myths and were largely ignorant of the hidden meaning they contained. Though separated from these ancient sages by time, the Presocratics had through a close contact with physical nature proceeded correctly in their pursuit of scientific knowledge. For this historical scheme, see Garner, "Francis Bacon, Natalis Comes and the Mythological Tradition," esp. 276-78, 291.

For Bacon's laments that the Presocratics existed only in fragments and his plan to collect them for thorough examination, see Farrington, 84, 116; *Advancement, Works*, III, 358, 365; *De augmentis*, IV, 358; V, 121.

[41]The others usually listed with these and Democritus are Pythagoras, Heraclitus, and Anaxagoras; see, e.g., Farrington, *The Philosophy of Francis Bacon*, 68, 84, 116, and *Works*, IV, 64, 72, 358.

[42]The brief survey that follows is not meant to be exhaustive, but rather indicative of Bacon's appropriation of these poets for his own scientific philosophy. That his knowledge of them goes far beyond the direct references examined here is clear, to take only one major work, in the *Advancement*; see, e.g., Weinberger's notes in *Science, Faith, and Politics*, on Hesiod (188), Empedocles (59-60), and Parmenides (68).

The best compact scholarly account of how the fragments of the Presocratics were preserved is Kirk et al., *The Presocratic Philosophers*, esp. 1-6. The most important sources for modern scholars are Plato, Aristotle, Simplicius, Plutarch, Sextus Empiricus, Clement of Alexandria, Hippolytus (theologian, third c. A.D.), Diogenes Laertius, and Stobaeus.

have served to caution him" against "founding a new school of philosophy" (Farrington, p. 117). Here Bacon is identifying the tendency of all philosophers, even the revered Presocratics, to create "systems," the Idols of the Theatre analyzed in *Novum Organum*; Gilbert's duly finds a place there (*Works*, IV, 65).

Though Bacon's few direct references to Xenophanes are perhaps in proportion to the number of surviving fragments, this scientific poet nevertheless exemplifies what Bacon admired among the Presocratics. In a note to *De augmentis*, Book VI, Chap. II, for example, Ellis cites a fragment of Xenophanes as "one of the earliest expressions" of the kind of genuine skepticism Bacon is discussing there (*Works*, I, 622; IV, 412), although Bacon himself makes no direct reference to Xenophanes in this context. Similarly, had Bacon known of another Xenophanic fragment, on fossils, he would have shared the admiration of modern commentators: "The deduction based upon fossils [that the sea dries up and preserves organisms in the mud] is a remarkable and impressive one. The enumeration of different occurrences [of this phenomenon] is in itself unusually scientific [for ca. 540 B.C.]."[43]

There can be no doubt, in any case, that Xenophanes' treatment of philosophical and scientific subjects in verse influenced Empedocles and Parmenides,[44] the two most important Presocratic scientific poets for Bacon. As noted above, these fifth-century writers were chiefly responsible for establishing philosophical and scientific poetry as a genre. In Bacon, they are referred to much more frequently than Xenophanes, and together their scientific ideas occupy Bacon more than those of any other Presocratic except Democritus.

Of Bacon's dozen or so direct references to Parmenides, four occur in the rolls of Presocratics who came nearer to the study of nature than Plato or Aristotle (*Works*, III, 365; IV, 358; Farrington, pp. 111, 116). Like Xenophanes, he is grouped with those "contemplators of nature" (including again Democritus) who were long-lived as a result of their admiration of the many and great wonders of the natural world (*Historia vitae et mortis*, V, 280). But Parmenides also appears at key moments in both the *Advancement*

---

[43]For this and another case of Xenophanes' scientific inductive reasoning, see Kirk et al., 176–77; the fragment cited by Ellis is no. 186 in Kirk, 179.

[44]See Kirk et al., *The Presocratic Philosophers*, 102–103, n. 1, and 166ff.

and *De augmentis*, where Bacon's central epistemological idea of the pyramid of knowledge, discussed above, is being defined:

For knowledges are as pyramids, whereof history and experience are the basis. And so of Natural Philosophy the basis is Natural History; the stage next the basis is Physic; the stage next the vertical point is Metaphysic. As for the cone and vertical point ("the work which God worketh from the beginning to the end" [Eccles. 3:11], namely, the summary law of nature) it may fairly be doubted whether man's inquiry can attain to it. But these three are the true stages of knowledge . . . And therefore the speculation was excellent in Parmenides and Plato (although in them it was but a bare speculation), "that all things by a certain scale ascend to unity."[45]

Most of Bacon's references to Parmenides, however, turn up in connection with the Italian natural philosopher Bernardino Telesio (1505–1588), whom Bacon saw as "reviving" the scientific theories of the Presocratic poet-philosopher. General comments to this effect are made in *De augmentis* and *Thema coeli* (*Works*, IV, 359; V, 551), but it is in the *De principiis* that Parmenides and Telesio figure most prominently. This unfinished work, possibly as late as 1624 but no earlier than 1609,[46] was meant to be an extended mythographical essay, of the kind found in *Wisdom of the Ancients* and in the examples of Parabolical Poesy in *De augmentis*, by which scientific ideas were allegorically expounded. Despite the promise of the work's full title ("On Principles and Origins, according to the Fables of Cupid and Coelum: or the Philosophy of Parmenides and Telesius and especially Democritus, treated in the Myth of Cupid"), the allegoresis of the Coelum myth was not completed for this work (it does appear in *Wisdom of the Ancients*), nor is Democritus discussed, except fleetingly. Telesio's theory, that heat and cold are the basic elements of the universe and explain all phenomena in the physical world, is the work's main concern,[47] but Bacon also seizes the opportunities afforded by Telesio's association with Parmenides to critique post-Socratic philosophy and science, and thus to define more clearly his own method.

---

[45]*Works*, IV, 361–62. Weinberger (248) identifies the source of this saying as Plato's *Parmenides* 165e2–66e5.

[46]See Rossi, 120–21, who argues for the later date.

[47]See Ellis's introduction to the Latin text, *Works*, III, 65–77; and G. Rees, "Matter Theory: An Unifying Factor in Bacon's Natural Philosophy," *Ambix* 24 (1977), 110–25.

In his exposition of "Cupid" or the atom, Bacon surveys various ancient philosophers on the constituents of matter. Among them was Parmenides, who

maintained two principles of things, fire and earth, or heaven and earth. For he asserted that the sun and stars were real fire, pure and limpid, not degenerate as fire is with us, which is only as Vulcan thrown down from heaven, and lamed by the fall. And these opinions of Parmenides Telesius has in our age revived; a man strong and well armed with the reasonings of the Peripatetics (if they were worth anything), which likewise he has turned against themselves; but embarrassed in his affirmations, and better at pulling down than at building up. Of the discoveries of Parmenides himself the account is very scanty and shadowy; yet the foundations of a similar opinion seem plainly laid in the book written by Plutarch on the "Primal Cold"; which appears to have been derived from some ancient treatise, at that time extant but now lost. (*Works*, V, 476)

The implicit contrast between the relatively simple matter theories of the Presocratic poet-philosopher and the dubious "reasonings" of the more speculative Peripatetics is a recurrent theme in the *De principiis*. After fifteen more pages of analysis of Telesio's theories, Bacon adds this comment, which shows how the influence of Aristotelian thought was detrimental to Telesio's adaptation of Parmenides: "Such then are the opinions of Telesius, and perhaps also of Parmenides, concerning the principles of things, except that Telesius has added something of his own respecting Hyle, being led astray by the Peripatetic notions" (*Works*, V, 490). A similar criticism is made two pages later, when Bacon is defending the reality of the atom ("which is a true being, having matter, form, dimension, place, resistance, appetite, motion, and emanations; which likewise, amid the destruction of all natural bodies, remains unshaken and eternal") as against some "imaginary" or "abstract principle," like Aristotle's *hyle*: "Telesius however chose *Hyle*, which, though the offspring of a later age, he transferred into the philosophy of Parmenides" (*Works*, V, 492).

Near the end of the *De principiis*, Bacon confronts directly the relationship between Parmenides and Telesio, and in so doing reveals the value of the scientific poet's theoretical physics:

to some it may perhaps seem scarce worthwhile to take such pains in refuting the philosophy of Telesius, a philosophy not much spoken of or received. But I do not stand upon such points of dignity. For of Telesius himself I have a good opinion, and acknowledge him as a lover of truth,

useful to the sciences, the reformer of certain opinions, and the first of
the moderns; at the same time it is not as Telesius that I have to do with
him, but as the restorer of the philosophy of Parmenides, to whom
much respect is due. But my principal reason for being more full in this
part is that in dealing with him who comes first, I take occasion to
discuss many questions which may be transferred to the refutation of
other sects, of which I shall have to treat hereafter; that I may not be
obliged to say the same things many times over. For errors, though
different, have their fibres strangely entangled and intertwined; yet so
that they may often be mowed down by one refutation as by a sweep of
a scythe. (*Works*, V, 495)

This passage tells us first that "much respect is due" to Parmenides, for the perspicacity of his investigation of nature, even
though his work is fragmentary and imperfect; and second, that
as Telesio anticipates other modern theories of matter, so Parmenides anticipated him. Hence, the *De principiis* is a characteristically Baconian analysis of a "sect" or system of philosophy, and
Parmenides is used to dismantle Telesio as Xenophanes had been
used to undermine Gilbert.

Parmenides is important, then, not because his theories are
correct, but because (1) his *method* was sounder than that of the
Peripatetics, and he can thus be used to show the weaknesses of
later Greek scientific speculation; and (2) his own theories, while
better grounded in experience than the Peripatetics', must nevertheless be seen as constituting a fledgling "system" of their own
and are therefore useful in evaluating modern successors like Telesio.[48] For his part, Telesio has gone one step farther in the
wrong direction by combining the abstract Aristotelian concept of
*hyle* with the more experientially based theories of Parmenides.

(That the *simplicity* of Parmenides' physics appealed to Bacon is
also evident in the *Historia ventorum*. When he examines "The
Local Origins of Winds," Bacon puzzles over those winds emanating from caverns, with specific examples from Derbyshire,
Wales, and Peru. Then follows this comment:

If the earth be the original source of cold, as Parmenides maintained (an
opinion not to be despised, seeing that cold and density are closely
united); it is not less probable that warm exhalations should be thrown

---

[48]At times, Bacon's preference for Presocratic physics over that of Aristotle and his followers is so extreme that he forgets to condemn their implicit "system building" (e.g.,
*Works* IV, 64); but at others, he regretfully sweeps them aside with his scythe, however
much more reliable they are than the Peripatetics (e.g., Farrington, 116–17).

up from the central cold of the earth, than that they should be thrown down from the cold of the upper air. (*Works*, V, 161)

Though brief, this is a rare and therefore significant instance of an ancient physical theory being cited in a Baconian "natural history."[49] It also highlights Bacon's preference for theories that are not hampered by unnecessary abstraction and that—unlike Telesio's—can be easily applied.)

The third Presocratic philosopher-poet, Empedocles, makes a somewhat less conspicuous appearance in Bacon's works than Parmenides, whose poem Empedocles emulated.[50] Though not mentioned by name in *Wisdom of the Ancients*, Empedocles has been identified as a major source or analogue for a number of cosmological notions, including that of man as microcosm, and for Bacon's own idea of the "ethereal spirit."[51] These are found in Bacon's scientific allegoresis of the myths of Coelum, Prometheus, and Proserpina, as well as in the *Historia vitae et mortis*.[52] It is curious that Bacon does not refer to Empedocles as the originator of the theory of the four elements, since Aristotle identifies him as such in the *Metaphysics*,[53] and since Bacon repeatedly attacks this ubiquitous theory, notably in *Novum Organum* (e.g., *Works*, IV, 55, 61). It is unthinkable that Bacon was unaware of the theory's origin, and we can only wonder why he does not mention Empedocles' poem in this connection. Bacon does, however, include Empedocles in four of his catalogs of the Presocratics deserving further study (*Works*, III, 365, and n. 1; Farrington, pp. 68, 111, 116), and at least two specific scientific ideas are directly attributed to him. There are two references, for example, to his second most celebrated notion (next to the four elements), the

---

[49]Parmenides is cited on the same point in Bacon's longest natural history, *Sylva sylvarum*, Century I, 69 (*Works*, II, 370). On the issue of citing authorities in natural histories, see Part V below, on Virgil.

[50]In addition to *On Nature* (perhaps 3,000 lines in length), Empedocles' poems are thought to include *Purifications* (perhaps 2,000 lines) and (according to Diogenes Laertius) 600 lines *On Medicine*, the latter completely lost (recall Aristotle's reference to "a [verse] treatise on medicine or natural science" in relation to Empedocles). Kirk et al. point out that Empedocles "wrote out of a deep preoccupation with Parmenides' thought," that his writings contain verbal echoes of Parmenides' poem, and that "Empedocles' fragments are more extensive than those of any other Presocratic" (282–83, which see also for the difficulty in establishing the canon). See also n. 3, above.

[51]See D. P. Walker, "Spirits in Francis Bacon," *Francis Bacon: Terminologia e Fortuna nel XVII Secolo*, Lessico Intellettuale Europeo XXXIII, ed. Marta Fattori (Roma: Edizioni dell'Ateneo, 1984), 315–27.

[52]See Lemmi, *The Classical Deities in Bacon*, 50, 76, 85, 133.

[53]See Kirk et al., p. 286, frag. 347.

theory of Strife and Friendship. This idea is praised in *Novum Organum* as one of the Presocratic notions (along with Democritus' atoms, Parmenides' "Heaven and Earth" and others) as having "some savour of the nature of things and experience, and bodies," as opposed to the mere "words of logic" in Aristotle's physics (*Works* IV, 64); and in the *De principiis* it is applied in passing to Telesio's primary elements of heat and cold (*Works* V, 489). The *Descriptio globi intellectualis,* in Bacon's consideration of various arguments on the material substance of the stars and planets, contains this reference to another Empedoclean notion, his explanation for the spots on the moon:

> though it be true that impure and feculent flames (of which kind of substance Empedocles thought the moon consisted) are unequal, yet the inequalities have no fixed places, but are commonly movable; whereas the spots in the moon are supposed to be constant. Besides, it is now ascertained by telescopes that these spots also have their own inequalities, so that the moon is found to be clearly of manifold configuration, and that selenography or map of the moon . . . seems now by the industry of Galileo and others to be nearly attained.[54]

Striking here is that Empedocles' theory, based on careful observation not only of the moon but of flames and fire (a subject of great interest to Bacon), is thought worth considering in relation to one of the most celebrated astronomical questions of the early seventeenth century. That it took Galileo's telescope to prove Empedocles wrong, as it were, indicates how seriously Bacon took the scientific ideas and observations in the surviving fragments of his poem.

Whether acknowledged or not, then, the scientific poems of the Presocratics served Bacon in both expository and argumentative capacities. They enabled him to evaluate the scientific theories and methodologies of others, and to articulate more clearly his own.

---

[54]*Works,* V, 535; Bacon's source for this Empedoclean fragment is identified as Stobaeus (*Works,* III, 760, n. 1).

## IV.  BACON AND LUCRETIUS

If Bacon regretted that only odd collections of disconnected quotations from Xenophanes, Parmenides, Empedocles, and the other Presocratics had come down the river of time, some reparation was to be found in the 7,500 lines of Lucretius' *De rerum natura*, the most important ancient scientific poem for the Renaissance.[55] Bacon repeatedly acknowledges it as one of the major repositories of information about the Presocratic philosophers (Farrington, *Philosophy*, pp. 68, 84, 116), and there are substantial passages on four of the seven Presocratics he usually cites: Anaxagoras (1.830–920, 2.865–930, 2.973–990), Heraclitus (1.635–704), Empedocles (1.716–829), and Democritus (3.371, 3.1039–41, 5.622).[56] One should note, too, that in reading Lucretius, Bacon could not but be aware of the antecedent tradition of scientific poetry, to which the *De rerum natura* was a conscious contribution.[57] It is, however, as a source of scientific ideas central to his own scientific philosophy—particularly those he attributed to Democritus—that Bacon makes use of Lucretius' poem.

Charles W. Lemmi has found Lucretius to be the source of many specific ideas in the scientific exposition of no fewer than five of the fables in *Wisdom of the Ancients*: Coelum, Cupid, Proserpina, Orpheus, and Prometheus.[58] The first of these, "Coelum;

---

[55]The manuscripts of Lucretius and Manilius were first rediscovered, after a thousand years of neglect, in 1417; the editio princeps of *De rerum natura* was 1473. A general study is George Depue Hadzsits, *Lucretius and His Influence* (New York: Cooper Square, 1963).

[56]These are the formal discussions and direct references, but there are of course many other places where Presocratic ideas are adopted (e.g., Democritus' atomic theory as modified by Epicurus) or where the Presocratic poet-philosophers are paraphrased or imitated (e.g., Empedocles at 1.25, 1.492–93, 5.101–103; see Loeb ed., *Lucretius: De Rerum Natura*, trans. W. H. D. Rouse, rev. Martin Ferguson Smith [Cambridge, Mass.: Harvard University Press, 1975], 4, 40–43, 387). It is difficult to know when Bacon relies on Lucretius (as opposed to Aristotle or some other intermediary) for the first three philosophers listed here; I have concentrated on Democritus for reasons that will become clear. For some of Bacon's non-scientific uses of Lucretius, see n. 38, above.

[57]That tradition includes not only Parmenides and Empedocles but also Aratus, via Cicero's verse translation; see Farrington, "Form and Purpose in the *De Rerum Natura*," in *Lucretius*, ed. D. R. Dudley, 19–34, esp. 19; and Maguinness, "The Language of Lucretius," 82ff. The Loeb editor says the most important Greek influences on Lucretius were Homer and Empedocles (liii).

[58]*The Classical Deities in Bacon*, 55, 61, 76, 84–85, 135–36, 153–54.

or the Origin of things," is presumably a version of the material originally intended for the *De principiis* (see full title, above, p. 29):

> This fable seems to be an enigma concerning the origin of things, not much differing from the philosophy afterwards embraced by Democritus: who more openly than any one else asserted the eternity of matter, while he denied the eternity of the world; a point in which he came somewhat nearer to the truth as declared in the divine narrative; for that represents matter without form as existing before the six days' works.[59]

Of particular interest here is the way that Democritus and Lucretius are linked, near the end of this allegorical exposition:

> Saturn is represented as thrust out and overthrown only, not as cut off and extinguished; because it was the opinion of Democritus that the world might yet relapse into its ancient confusion and intervals of no government: an event which Lucretius prayed might not happen in his own times.
> Which may all-ruling Fortune keep far hence,
> And reason teach it, not experience. (*Works*, VI, 724)

While the connection between Democritus and Lucretius in this passage may seem fortuitous, it in fact signals a habit of mind by which Bacon repeatedly relies on the Roman poet as a spokesman for the Presocratic who "penetrated more shrewdly and deeply into nature" than Aristotle.[60] This habit, which operates strikingly in a number of works, will illustrate the extent to which Lucretius' poem penetrated Bacon's thinking.[61]

The title of Bacon's *Cogitationes de natura rerum* (1604) perhaps only coincidentally recalls that of Lucretius' poem; it is, however, a straightforward exposition of the Democritean ideas that Bacon found so rife in Lucretius. Spedding, for example, locates an opinion attributed to Democritus—that "all things may be made out of all things"—in *De rerum natura* 1.782–88, where Democritus himself is not mentioned.[62] If we look a few pages later in both

---

[59]*Works*, VI, 723. The reference to the "divine narrative" anticipates the concluding paragraph of "Coelum," which is careful to give final authority on the question of "origins" to Genesis and to identify Democritus' theories as mere "oracles of sense which have long since ceased and failed" (VI, 725).

[60]*Redargutio philosophorum* (Farrington, 116); similar assertions are made in *Cogitata et visa* (Farrington, 84) and *Advancement* (*Works*, III, 358).

[61]For the importance of Democritean ideas generally in Bacon, see Rossi, 53 et passim; on the question of Bacon's apparent rejection of atomism (noticeably in *Novum Organum*) and for some different interpretations of this, see Jardine, 113–14.

[62]*Works*, III, 18 n. 2; V, 422. All line references to and translations from Lucretius given here are from the Loeb ed.; line references in *Works* sometimes differ.

Lucretius and in Bacon, we find an even more striking expression of the same idea, and a case of Bacon's indebtedness that has not, I think, been noticed before. In Chap. IV of *Cogitationes*, "On the common Division of Motion, that it is useless and rude," Bacon is arguing that the business of science is to discover the means of exciting or stopping every kind of motion, "and thereby to preserve, change, and transform bodies." In order to achieve this kind of control over nature, however, one must first understand

those motions . . . which are simple, primitive, and fundamental, whereof the rest are composed. For it is most certain that by how much the more simple motions are discovered, by so much will the power of man be increased and made independent of materials special and prepared, and strengthened for the production of new works. Surely as the words or terms of all languages, in an immense variety, are composed of a few simple letters, so all the actions and powers of things are formed by a few natures and original elements of simple motions. And it were shame that men should have examined so carefully the tinklings of their own voice, and should yet be so ignorant of the voice of nature; and as in the early ages (before letters were invented), should discern only compound sounds and words, not distinguishing the elements and letters. (*Works*, V, 426)

This same analogy between letters and atoms, as between words and compound bodies, appears no fewer than five times in *De rerum natura*. The context of the second occurrence reveals how, for both Lucretius and Bacon, the analogy reinforces the scientific theory to which both writers ascribe, Democritus' belief that "all things may be made out of all things":

And it is often of great importance with what and in what position these same first-beginnings are held together, and what motions they impart and receive mutually; for the same beginnings constitute sky, sea, earth, rivers, sun, the same make crops, trees, animals, but they move differently mixed with different elements and in different ways. Moreover, all through these very lines of mine you see many elements common to many words, although you must confess that lines and words differ one from another both in meaning and in the sound of their soundings. So much can elements do, when nothing is changed but order; but the elements that are the beginnings of things can bring with them more kinds of variety, from which all the various things can be produced.[63]

Bacon's elaboration of Lucretius' metaphor is characteristic of his ironic attacks on philosophical systems, especially in the caustic references to the "tinklings" of men's own voices which they prefer to "the voice of nature." While Lucretius refers self-consciously to the letters, words, and lines of his poem, Bacon contrasts the vain words of philosophy with those of the Book of Nature, which can be fully understood only by analyzing the very letters that make them up—in this context, the atoms of Democritus. Bacon's unacknowledged appropriation of this Lucretian metaphor, here and elsewhere,[64] is a testimony to Lucretius' success as a scientific poet. Just as interesting here, though, is the fact that neither of the Lucretian passages imbedded in the *Cogitationes* contains a direct reference to Democritus; Bacon, in expounding the Presocratic's themes, merely relies on the Roman poet. This is to happen again and again.

---

[63] atque eadem magni refert primordia saepe
cum quibus et quali positura contineantur
et quos inter se dent motus accipiantque;
namque eadem caelum mare terras flumina solem
constituunt, eadem fruges arbusta animantis,
verum aliis alioque modo commixta moventur.
quin etiam passim nostris in versibus ipsis
multa elementa vides multis communia verbis,
cum tamen inter se versus ac verba necessest
confiteare et re et sonitu distare sonanti.
tantum elementa queunt permutato ordine solo;
at rerum quae sunt primordia, plura adhibere
possunt unde queant variae res quaeque creari. (1.817–29)
The other passages are 1.196–97, 912–14; 2.688–90, 1013–18. The last instance is especially graphic in relation to Bacon's use of the metaphor: "Moreover, it is important in my own verses with what and in what order the various elements are placed. For the same letters denote sky, sea, earth, rivers, sun, the same denote crops, trees, animals. If they are not all alike, yet by far the most part are so; but position marks the difference in what results. So also when we turn to real things: when the combinations of matter, when its motions, order, position, shapes are changed, the thing also must be changed" (Loeb ed., p. 173–75).
The Loeb editor notes that "both the Latin *elementa* and the Greek [*stoicheia*] can mean both physical elements and the letters of the alphabet" (p. 68, n. *a*). Of this Bacon is clearly aware; his original Latin text of the passage quoted above concludes, "Turpe autem fuerit hominibus, propriae vocis tintinnabula tam accurate explorasse, ad naturae autem vocem tam illiteratos esse; et more prisci seculi (antequam literae inventae essent) sonos tantum compositos et voces dignoscere, elementa et literas non distinguere" (*Works*, III, 22).
[64] Though Bacon modifies it for special purposes in *Novum Organum* (1610), the metaphor still carries with it the associations of Democritean atomism: "So also the letters of the alphabet in themselves and apart have no use or meaning, yet they are the subject-matter for the composition and apparatus of all discourse. So again the seeds of things are of much latent virtue, and yet of no use except in their development" (*N.O.*, I, CXXI; *Works*, IV, 107, on experiments of light).

In the *Descriptio globi intellectualis* (written ca. 1612)[65] a number
of passages have analogues in Lucretius. Spedding points out,
for example, that "We find in Lucretius nearly the same views [on
astronomy] as those of Bacon" (*Works*, III, 720). He cites *De rerum
natura* 5.622ff., a passage that begins "For among the most likely
causes [for the apparent courses of sun, moon, and stars] is that
which the venerable judgement of that great man Democritus
puts forward" (Loeb ed., p. 427). Spedding goes on to say that
Bacon probably got his ideas not from Lucretius, but from Telesio. However, the many references to Democritus in this work,
along with Bacon's tendency to identify Lucretian with Democritean ideas, suggests that he may have simply relied on the *De
rerum natura* in this case, too. One of Democritus' ideas in the
*Descriptio* has to do with the infinity of matter and space, and the
existence of the vacuum:

For in the opinion of Democritus vacuity is bounded and circumscribed,
so that beyond certain limits distraction or divulsion of bodies is no
more possible than compulsion or compaction. For although in those
works of Democritus which have come down to us this is never ex-
pressly declared, yet he seems to imply as much when he asserts that
bodies as well as spaces are infinite: using as his argument, that otherwise (that is, if space were infinite and bodies finite) bodies would never
cohere. Therefore by reason of matter and space being equally infinite,
vacuity is necessarily confined within certain bounds, which seems to
have been his real opinion rightly understood; that is, that there is a
certain limit to the expansion of bodies by reason of the vacuum with
which they are coupled; and that there is no solitary vacuum, not en-
closed in a body.[66]

Here Bacon claims to infer a coherent technical theory from the
fragments of Democritus. But on which "works" does he base
this reconstruction? Spedding's note on the first sentence in this
quotation refers the reader to Lucretius 1.984ff., a passage in
which Democritus is not mentioned, but in which all the ideas
Bacon attributes to him here appear:

Besides, if all the space in the universe stood contained within fixed
boundaries on all sides and were limited, by this time the store of mat-

---

[65]For dating and an introduction, see *Works*, III, 715. This unfinished work was composed between the *Advancement* and the *De augmentis* and is, like them, a survey of existing knowledge; a good portion of it, however, is devoted to astronomy as one division of
natural philosophy.

[66]*Works*, V, 520. For Bacon's own ambivalence regarding the vacuum, see Rossi, 53, 100,
259 n. 59.

ter would by its solid weight have run together from all sides to the bottom, nor could anything be done under the canopy of heaven, nor would heaven exist at all or the sun's light, because assuredly all matter would be lying in a heap from sinking down through infinite ages past. But as it is, sure enough no rest is given to the bodies of the first-beginnings, because there is no bottom whatsoever, for them to run together as it were into it and fix their abode there. Always the business of the universe is going on with incessant motion in every part, and the elements of matter are being supplied from beneath, rushing from infinite space. (Loeb ed., p. 83).

Democritus' views on the vacuum are thus reconstituted from Lucretius' account of it.

That Bacon sees Lucretius as conveying unproblematically Democritus' scientific ideas is also clear a few pages earlier in the *Descriptio*, when he raises the question of whether there is a "system" in the heavens: "that is, whether the world or universe compose together one globe, with a centre; or whether the particular globes of earth and stars be scattered dispersedly, each on its own roots, without any system or common centre?" Here he actually identifies Democritus with Epicurus, the real hero of *De rerum natura*:

Certainly the school of Democritus and Epicurus boasted that their founders had overthrown the walls of the world; yet this did not absolutely follow from their words. For when Democritus had set down matter or seeds as infinite in quantity and finite in attributes and power, as moving about, and never located in any position from all eternity, he was driven by the very force of this opinion to constitute multiform worlds, subject to birth and death, some well ordered, others badly put together, even essays of worlds and vacant spaces between. (*Works*, V, 514–15)

Bacon goes on to take issue with this "school," which he has in fact constructed from the scraps of Democritus and the poem of Lucretius.[67] It would be unfair, of course, to blame Bacon for not distinguishing between the scientific theories of Democritus and the philosophy of Epicurus. As already noted, Bacon was a pioneer in his study of the Presocratics,[68] and even the ancients were capable of reading Epicurean atomism back into Democritus.[69]

---

[67]In his note to the Latin text, Spedding refers us to *De rerum natura* 1.73 (the praise of Epicurus) and 1.957 (on the infinity of the universe) (*Works*, III, 737, n. 2).

[68]See Farrington, 48, 111 n. 1.

[69]For three such instances involving Simplicius, Diogenes Laertius, and Aetius, see Kirk et al., 415 n. 1, 418 n. 1, 422–25.

Moreover, Lucretius himself does not always accurately represent even Epicurus' atomic theories.[70]

But the extent of Bacon's tendency to read Lucretius' poem as a compendium of Democritean physics is nevertheless significant. The *De principiis et originibus*, the work on atomism, Parmenides, and Telesio discussed above, offers an excellent further example. Early in his allegorical exposition of the myth of Cupid, Bacon explains that Cupid (the atom) is represented as an egg hatched by Nox because knowledge of the physically imperceptible atom can be gained only "by exclusions and negatives: and proof made by exclusion is a kind of ignorance, and as it were night, with regard to the thing included." The rest of the passage, given below, incorporates two direct quotations from the first book of *De rerum natura*. The first is from Lucretius' refutation of Heraclitus' view that all things are composed ultimately of fire (687–89), the second from a refutation of the four elements of Empedocles and his followers (778–80). Bacon gives both quotations as though they were Democritus' own words:

Whence Democritus excellently affirmed that atoms or seeds, and the virtue thereof, were unlike anything that could fall under the senses; but distinguished them as being of a perfectly dark and hidden nature; saying of themselves, "that they resembled neither fire nor anything else that could be felt or touched;" and of their virtue, "that in the generation of things the first beginnings must needs have a dark and hidden nature, lest something should rise up to resist and oppose them." Atoms therefore are neither like sparks of fire, nor drops of water, nor bubbles of air, nor grains of dust, nor particles of spirit or ether.[71]

A few sentences later, Bacon finds a discrepancy between Democritus' supposed views on the motion and gravity of the atom,

---

[70]For inaccuracies in *De rerum natura*, see Kirk et al., 423. The fullest study of this relationship is Diskin Clay, *Lucretius and Epicurus* (Ithaca: Cornell University Press, 1983). A good general survey of the scientific ideas in the poem is O. E. Lowenstein, "The Pre-Socratics, Lucretius, and Modern Science," *Lucretius*, ed. D. R. Dudley, 1–18.

[71]*Works*, V, 463–64. Bacon also quotes Democritus on the insensibility of atoms in the *Sylva sylvarum*; Ellis's note (*Works*, II, 381) refers the reader to Sextus Empiricus and Aristotle's *De anima* for possible sources, but many of the details of Bacon's discussion (e.g., the analogy between atoms and motes in a sunbeam) suggest that Bacon may again be conflating Lucretius with Democritus; compare the passage with *De rerum natura* 2.112–41, 308–16, 834–41.

and the ancient wisdom which he is extracting from the fable
of Cupid:

For Democritus is found to be not only at variance with the parable, but
inconsistent and almost in contradiction with himself in that which he
says further on this point. For he should have attributed to the atom a
heterogeneous motion, as well as a heterogeneous body and a heterogeneous virtue; whereas, out of the motions of the larger bodies, he has
selected two motions; namely, the descent of heavy things and the ascent of light (which latter he explained as the effect of force or percus-
sion of the heavier driving the less heavy upwards), and ascribed them
as primitive motions to the atom. (*Works*, V, 465)

As Ellis points out, the last part of this statement paraphrases *De
rerum natura* 2.83–85, but in a footnote Bacon's exasperated editor
explains how his author's mental habit has led him into factual
error: "But Democritus himself did not ascribe gravity to the
atom, and in this as in some other points Bacon was misled by
assuming that Lucretius always represents the opinions of Democritus."[72] Exactly how Bacon arrived at this position (recall that
Democritus is mentioned by name only twice in scientific contexts in *De rerum natura*), we do not know. But these examples
show not just that Bacon knew Lucretius' poem extremely well
(these many allusions and quotations are presumably made from
memory), but that he relied on it as a (largely unacknowledged)
source for the ideas of the Presocratic philosopher whom he considered the most important scientific thinker of antiquity.

---

[72]*Works*, III, 83 n. 1. Another direct quotation from Lucretius occurs later in the *De
principiis* (*Works*, V, 476), but without attribution to either Democritus or Lucretius; here
Bacon uses the quotation to refute all the Presocratics who held that there was but one
constitutent of matter, whether air, water, or fire (the same point is expanded in the "Pan"
of *De augmentis*). The same two lines cited here appear no fewer than four times in *De
rerum natura* (1.670–71, 792–93; 2.753–54; 3.519–20). The first two of these appearances
occur within a few lines of three passages quoted elsewhere by Bacon (1.687–89, 1.778–80,
and 1.782–88, discussed above).

## V. BACON'S SCIENCE AND VIRGIL'S POETRY

Never, as we saw in Part II, does Bacon's discussion of poetic theory or poetic genres confront the issue of scientific poetry, or even acknowledge the poems of Xenophanes, Parmenides, Empedocles or Lucretius. Nor, as the preceding surveys of his various citations and appropriations of them in scientific contexts witness, does he ever refer to them as verse-writers, much less as poets. The deliberateness of these omissions can be inferred from Bacon's treatment of Lucretius, whose long poem was available to him intact and whom he cites more often than the others. When he appears in a purely illustrative or rhetorical capacity, Lucretius is accorded the laurel (e.g., *Advancement, Works* III, 317-18: "the poet Lucretius describeth elegantly"; *Novum Organum, Works* IV, 113-14: "as well sang the poet"; and *Essays, Works* VI, 378: "The poet . . . saith . . . excellently well"). But as there is supposedly no room at all for "elegance" or "singing"—or, of course, for "the poet"—in the serious business of science, no such references appear in any of the scientific contexts where Lucretius is cited. (Interestingly, this pattern can also be observed in Aristotle, who in the *Poetics* discusses Empedocles "by custom" as a poet, but who in his scientific writings tends to cite him only for his scientific ideas, without reference to the fact that *On Nature* is a poem.[73])

But in the case of Virgil, whom Bacon probably cites "more than any other writer in any field ancient or modern,"[74] matters are necessarily different. While he, too, is avoided in Bacon's poetic theory, and while Bacon frequently cites him in scientific contexts without acknowledgment, direct quotations from (or even

---

[73]Of the 14 Aristotelian references to Empedocles (from a total of seven different scientific treatises) given in Kirk et al., only one has any reference to Empedocles' work as a poem, and there it is for a striking analogy: "And Empedocles puts this well in his poem, when he says, 'Thus do tall trees bear eggs: first olives . . .'; for the egg is a foetus . . ." (frag. 385, p. 306).

[74]Charles Whitney, *Francis Bacon and Modernity* (New Haven: Yale University Press, 1986), 171.

veiled allusions to) Virgil's poems were much more likely to be recognized by Bacon's readers. Moreover, Bacon could hardly question Virgil's status as a great poet—not even if the *Georgics* were his only poem. What, then, are we to make of the profusion of Virgilian citations in Bacon's scientific and philosophical writings? If we again exclude quotations that seem to have mainly a rhetorical or stylistic function (see n. 38 above), we are left with a substantial number of Virgilian passages cited for their scientific import. A study of these yields three striking conclusions: (1) While Bacon clearly recognized that Virgil wrote in the direct tradition of Lucretius, he is just as likely to bring in the "mimetic" poems—*Eclogues* or *Aeneid*—as sources of scientific observations or theories, as he is to cite the *Georgics* for such purposes. (2) On this evidence a case can be made that Bacon, to an extent at least, participates in the ancient tradition of reading Virgil as one of the *learned* poets whose works are compendia of all kinds of knowledge. Ironically, Bacon thus returns to the very habit of mind which had sparked Plato's attack on mimetic poetry in the first place: the age-old association of Poetry and Knowledge. (3) Finally, in his appropriations of material from Virgil's mimetic poems, Bacon tacitly ignores the strict divisions between Reason and Imagination, and between science and poetry, that he so carefully and anxiously constructs in his theoretical statements on the hierarchy of human knowledge. The mimetic poetry of Virgil's "imagination" merges all too easily with the discursive philosophy of Bacon's "reason."

One key to Bacon's reading—and his consequent scientific appropriation—of Virgil lies in his own perception of a continuity between Virgil's poems and the scientific poem of Lucretius. This can be seen, interestingly enough, in the way Bacon deploys a key quotation from the *Eclogues* in his allegorical exposition of the Pan myth in *Wisdom of the Ancients*.

"Pan" is the fable that explains in small Bacon's whole philosophy of science, while making a strong case for Democritean atomic physics; Bacon signaled its importance by later enlarging the *Wisdom* version (1609) for *De augmentis* (1623). The connection between Lucretius and Virgil is most apparent in a direct quotation from *Eclogues* 6.31-34, where the sage Silenus is forced by Chromis, Mnasyllos, and Aegle to sing the songs he had promised but never delivered. The first of these songs is on the origins

of things, and Bacon cites it in the opening paragraph of his allegorical explanation of the origin of matter:

Pan, as the very word declares, represents the universal frame of
things, or Nature. About his origin there are and can be but two opinions; for Nature is either the offspring of Mercury—that is of the Divine
Word (an opinion which the Scriptures establish beyond question, and
which was entertained by all the more divine philosophers); or else of
the seeds of things mixed and confused together. For they who derive
all things from a single principle, either take that principle to be a God,
or if they hold it to be a material principle, assert it to be though actually
one yet potentially many; so that all difference of opinion on this point
is reducible to one or other of these two heads,—the world is sprung
either from Mercury, or from all the suitors. He sang, says Virgil,
   How through the void of space the seeds of things
   Came first together; seeds of the sea, land, air,
   And the clear fire; how from these elements
   All embryos grew, and the great world itself
   Swelled by degrees and gathered in its globe. (Works, VI, 709)

The Lucretian substance of this passage, says one Virgilian
commentator, "has been noticed too often to require elaboration"; another calls these lines "the most important Lucretian
imitation in the Eclogues."[75] Bacon, whose exposition of Democritean atomism in "Coelum" was discussed above (pp. 34–35), certainly recognized the reiteration of this matter-theory in the
passage he quotes from Eclogue 6. For one thing, his exposition of
"Pan" proceeds, in a way similar to that in "Coelum," to reconcile
the two theories discussed here: "For true it is that this Pan,
whom we behold and contemplate and worship only too much,
is sprung from the Divine Word, through the medium of confused matter (which itself is God's creature) . . ."[76] Second, Bacon's revision of "Pan" in De augmentis suggests that, in the
original version just cited, he was relying on Virgil's paraphrase
of Lucretius' atomic cosmogony to stand in for that of Democritus. For, instead of repeating the Virgil quotation, the revision
extends the account of early matter-theories and mentions specifically "the doctrine of atoms invented by Leucippus, and sedu-

---

[75]William Berg, Early Virgil (London: Athlone Press, 1974), 182; Paul Alpers, The Singer
of the Eclogues: A Study of Virgilian Pastoral (Berkeley: University of California Press,
1979), 242.

[76]Works, VI, 709; see the similar maneuver in the discussion of "Coelum" and note 59,
above.

lously followed out by Democritus."[77] The excerpt from *Eclogue* 6 is deleted only because it is now superfluous.[78]

Today *Eclogue* 6 (a total of 86 lines) is viewed as a *Kataloggedicht*, a kind of inventory of poetic themes and forms, or a series of allusions to the poetic models in which Virgil found inspiration.[79] Virgil's tribute to Lucretius (lines 31–40) is only the most obvious of these, one more fully and directly expressed later in the *Georgics*.[80] Bacon himself, in quoting the first four of these lines for his own purpose, must have recognized the continuity between the two greatest scientific poets of antiquity. This point is further supported in that the single passage from the *Georgics* (2.492–94) which most eloquently acknowledges Virgil's debt to Lucretius[81] is cited elsewhere in *Wisdom of the Ancients*, though in a non-scientific context.[82] If, then, Virgil's debt to Lucretius in both the *Eclogues* and *Georgics* was apparent to Bacon, what uses did he make of Virgil's own scientific poem?

The general importance of the *Georgics* for Bacon, first of all, is clear not only from the many direct quotations but also from the "georgic vision" which Anthony Low has recently identified as

---

[77]In this instance, Bacon actually prefers the positions of Plato and Aristotle (whose theories he goes on to contrast with those of various Presocratics), because they come closer to explicating the part of the Pan myth with which he is here concerned, and because they are more consistent with his own need to see the "presence of the divine will" in the ordering of matter (see Garner, "Francis Bacon, Natalis Comes and the Mythological Tradition," 282, 286).

[78]In his revision, Bacon adds another verse quotation, a simile from *Aeneid* 6.270–71, to explain how Pan's seduction of the Moon is an allegory of "the intercourse of sense with heavenly or divine things" (IV, 327). His purpose here is to reinforce God's role in the disposition of matter; see the preceding note.

[79]Berg, *Early Virgil*, 182. For example, Hesiod, the primordial Greek didactic poet whose *Works and Days* obviously influenced the *Georgics*, is alluded to in *Eclogues* 6.70. Bacon of course would recognize this reference.

[80]For the influence of Lucretius (as well as Hesiod, Xenophanes, Empedocles, Nicander, and Aratus among the Greek scientific poets) on the *Georgics*, see L. P. Wilkinson, *The Georgics of Virgil: A Critical Survey* (Cambridge: Cambridge University Press, 1969), esp. Chap. 3.

[81]Thus D. E. W. Wormell, "The Personal World of Lucretius," *Lucretius*, ed. D. R. Dudley, 64–65.

[82]In the moral allegory of "Prometheus; or the State of Man," fortitude
   comes of Wisdom, which is as the Sun, and of meditation upon the inconstancy and fluctuations of human life, which is as the navigation of the ocean: two things which Virgil has well coupled together in those lines:—
   Ah, happy, could we but the causes know
   Of all that is! Then should we know no fears:
   Then should the inexorable Fate no power
   Possess to shake us, nor the jaws of death. (*Works*, VI, 752)
These same verses appear in *Advancement*, Book I, where Virgil is said "excellently and profoundly [to] couple the knowledge of causes and the conquest of all fears together as *concomitantia*" (III, 315).

fundamental to the entire Baconian scientific program. In this analysis, Bacon found in Virgil's Jupiter theodicy a new way of interpreting the curse of labor laid on fallen man in Genesis 3:19. Hence Bacon's philosophy emphasizes the positive value of work and the power that science confers on man. Moreover, the "Georgics of the Mind," which Bacon enunciates in the *Advancement* and *De augmentis*, can be seen as a revolutionary ideal which is at once philosophical, moral, cultural, and scientific.[83] Such an analysis is a salutary reminder that Baconian "science" is by no means cut off from the larger philosophical concerns which had always impinged on "natural philosophy" (and which, of course, likewise impinged on the ancient scientific poems we have been discussing).

But if Virgil's theme of "labor omnia vicit" (*Georgics* 1.145) provided Bacon with a conceptual framework for his scientific philosophy, how did he perceive the *Georgics* as a poem? With no formal account of scientific poetry to rely on, we must turn to two comments in the *Advancement* and *De augmentis* which constitute Bacon's only direct evaluation of Virgil as poet and of the *Georgics* as poem. The first is a thoroughly commonplace and off-hand assertion that Virgil is "the best poet . . . that to the memory of man [is] known" (*Works*, III, 274). The second, however, is this glowing claim: "Virgil promised himself, (and indeed obtained,) . . . as much glory of eloquence, wit, and learning in the expressing of the observations of husbandry, as of the heroical acts of Aeneas" (*Works*, III, 419; V, 5, citing *Georgics* 3. 289-290). Even if this cannot quite be taken at face value, it reveals two important points. First, by describing the *Georgics* as Virgil's "expressing [in verse] of the observations of husbandry," Bacon shows that he—like most English readers of the period—considered the *Georgics* to be a didactic poem containing practical, technical information on agriculture.[84] But his other assertion, that in writing it Virgil gained "as much glory of eloquence, wit, and learning . . . as of the heroical acts of Aeneas," makes it clear

---

[83]Anthony Low, *The Georgic Revolution* (Princeton: Princeton University Press, 1985), esp. 125-35, 139-43.

[84]The same was true of Hesiod, whose *Works and Days* was referred to as "*Hesiodus in hys Georgicks* or books of Husbandry" by William Webbe in 1586 (ed. Smith, *Elizabethan Critical Essays*, I, 238), and as *The Georgicks of Hesiod* by his learned English translator, George Chapman (London, 1618). Chapman also claims that Virgil, "among so many writers of *Georgicks*, only imitated" Hesiod (sig. A3v). Webbe and Chapman thus solved the problem of Hesiod's "nameless genre" by turning Virgil's title into a generic name and then anachronistically applying it to Hesiod.

that the *Georgics* is just as worthy—*as a poem*—as the *Aeneid*. It is precisely both poems' general qualities of "eloquence, wit, and learning"—rather than, as Bacon's formal poetic theory would have it, the treatment of mimetic subject matter—that qualify their author *as poet*. Furthermore, behind the comment about "eloquence, wit, and learning" lies the ancient view of the poet, decried by Plato, as primarily a teacher—of both facts and values, with little distinction being made between them.[85]

To claim that Bacon sees Virgil in the tradition of the "learned poet" is not, of course, to say that he naively attributes to him the kind of universal knowledge (including magic and prophecy) that was commonly thought to be his in the Middle Ages, and which was still being claimed for Homer, Ovid, and Virgil by some Renaissance syncretists and allegorists. This is clear from an ironical reference in the *Advancement* to "certain critics [who] are used to say hyperbolically, *That if all sciences were lost, they might be found in Virgil*" (III, 310). What I am suggesting, though, is that while on the one hand Bacon would theoretically deny that the *Georgics* was Poesy at all (because it didactically sets out "observations of husbandry"), on the other, he treats *all* of Virgil's major poems—mimetic and didactic alike—as collections of accurate "observations" about the natural world, and as sources for certain scientific ideas. Some indication of this has already been given above in the discussion of the *Eclogues*, but what Bacon means by Virgil's "wit and learning" can be seen perhaps most clearly in his deployment of various quotations in one particular genre of his scientific writings, the "natural history."

Let us begin with a characteristic passage from the *Historia ventorum*, Bacon's first natural history. Here is the last of twenty-six specific observations on "The Motions of Winds":

We should not altogether neglect the testimony of Virgil, seeing he was by no means ignorant of natural philosophy; "At once the winds rush

---

Had Bacon wished to de-emphasize the didactic element in the *Georgics*, he could have joined those who, like Seneca, claimed that Virgil's intention was to delight readers, not to instruct farmers. See Schuler and Fitch, esp. 18–19, 23–24, 37–38 n. 61.

Modern views on the genre or "true nature" of the poem range from Wilkinson, that "[i]f the *Georgics* has to be assigned to a *genre*, it is Descriptive Poetry" (*The Georgics of Virgil*, 4), to David O. Ross, Jr., *Virgil's Elements: Physics and Poetry in the Georgics* (Princeton: Princeton University Press, 1987), who argues that the *Georgics* "is a poem of science and uses the intellectual structures of scientific literature" (6).

[85]For a sketch of this tradition from antiquity to the Renaissance, see Schuler and Fitch, 4–5, 22–23; and Schuler, "Theory and Criticism of the Scientific Poem," esp. 32–39.

forth, the east, and south, and south-west laden with storms" [*Aeneid* 1.85]; and again, "I have seen all the battles of the winds meet together in the air" [*Georgics* 1.318]. So far then have I inquired concerning the motions of the winds in nature. I must now look to their motion in machines of human invention; and above all in the sails of ships. (*Works* V, 178–79)

In order to understand exactly how Bacon is using these quotations, we must first recall what he means by "natural history" and then scrutinize the key word "testimony" in his statement about Virgil's knowledge of natural philosophy. Ideally, a natural history for Bacon is

an uncritical record of observations of natural phenomena, which corresponds to the store in the memory of primitive sense-perceptions. This means that the observations it contains are to be recorded without embellishment, without bias, and without supporting citations from classical sources, as concisely and perspicuously as possible.[86]

Although in some of his instructions for the compilation of such histories Bacon seems to allow the inclusion of observations or conjectures derived from published sources (so long as they are carefully identified and handled), in the *Parasceve* he lays down, as a first warning, this injunction against wasted effort which "adds little or nothing" to a true natural history:

First then, away with antiquities, and citations or testimonies of authors; also with disputes and controversies and differing opinions; everything in short which is philological. Never cite an author except in a matter of doubtful credit: never introduce a controversy unless in a matter of great moment. And for all that concerns ornaments of speech, similitudes, treasury of eloquence, and such like emptinesses, let it be utterly dismissed. Also let all those things which are admitted be themselves set down briefly and concisely, so that they may be nothing less than words. For no man who is collecting and storing up materials for ship-building or the like, thinks of arranging them elegantly, as in a shop, and displaying them so as to please the eye; all his care is that they be sound and good, and that they be so arranged as to take up as little room as possible in the warehouse. And this is exactly what should be done here. (*Works*, IV, 254–55)

[86]Jardine, 135. My account of the "natural history" is indebted to the material excellently assembled by Jardine, 135–41. Key texts are the "Description of a Natural and Experimental History" (*Works*, IV, 251–63), the "Catalogue of Particular Histories by Titles" (IV, 265–70), and "The Natural and Experimental History . . . Being the Third Part of the Instauratio Magna" (V, 125ff.), which includes an introduction and the first six histories begun by Bacon.

It would be easy to show the extent to which Bacon himself fails to meet these criteria. His own penchant for analogous thinking and metaphor—exemplified here in the ship-builder—has been well documented by Brian Vickers; some of the natural histories even employ the traditional divisions of rhetorical arrangement.[87] And Jardine has shown that Bacon himself "could never resist interspersing the histories with conjectural explanations of the phenomena, despite his avowed intention to subordinate all examination of material to the task of preparing it for application of the inductive method."[88]

Are we, then, to see the "testimonies" of Virgil in the *Historia ventorum* as useless "antiquities" or "citations," or as "ornaments . . . of eloquence"—in short, as examples of Bacon's failure to compile a true natural history? I do not think so. On several occasions in the *Historia ventorum*, it is true, Bacon brings up only to dismiss as useless certain metaphors of "poets": those, for example, who "in their descriptions of the deluge represent the north wind as at that time imprisoned, and the south wind let loose with full powers" (*Works*, V, 154), or those who (like Virgil himself in *Aeneid* 1.50ff.) "have feigned that the kingdom of Aeolus was situated in subterranean dens and caverns, where the winds were imprisoned, and whence they were occasionally let loose" (*Works*, V, 160). Similarly, he disposes of those "theologians . . . who were likewise philosophers" who misinterpret metaphors having to do with the winds in Scripture (V, 160); and he strikes a double blow against the "imaginative" origins of alchemy by quoting from a Latin Paracelsian *poem* that in effect reduces the four points of the compass to three, in order to make all things accord with the "three principles" of Paracelsus.[89]

But the point here is not that poets' metaphors or images *per se* have no place in a natural history, but that they must be accurate in their representation of nature. Hence, even though personification operates in both the Virgilian quotations with which we

---

[87]Brian Vickers, *Francis Bacon and Renaissance Prose* (Cambridge: Cambridge University Press, 1968), 51–52 et passim.

[88]Jardine, 140 n. 1. Charles Whitney claims that Bacon's natural histories "do seem, in a kind of muddling way, to reflect his reportorial ideal" (*Francis Bacon and Modernity*, 133), and that in the histories Bacon "abandons the 'cultivation' of knowledge entirely" (135); but the examples given (134) are highly selective.

[89]*Works* V, 154; the untitled poem in question, identified by Spedding only by author, is by Johannes Pratensis and appears at the end of Petrus Severinus' *Idea medicinae philosophiae, fundamenta continens totius doctrinae Paracelsicae, Hippocraticae, & Galenicae* (Basle, 1571), excerpt quoted by Bacon on sig. GG3r (British Library copy 543.c.41). In *De augmentis* Bacon similarly associates the "fancies" of "astrological insanity" with a poetry whose "Muses be . . . old women," as he quotes an as yet unidentified Latin astrological poem (IV, 355).

began ("winds rush forth, . . . laden with storms"; "the battles of the winds meet"), these are presented as precise observations of the "motions of winds." Note, furthermore, how carefully and deliberately the authoritative source of these quotations is introduced: "We should not altogether neglect the testimony of Virgil, seeing he was by no means ignorant of natural philosophy." The "wit and learning" of Virgil are specified as knowledge of natural philosophy, and Bacon's use of a double litotes emphasizes the weight to be given the quotations that follow.[90] In addition, the context and the actual substance of these (and other) observations of nature suggest that they—like Virgil's "observations of husbandry"—are to be treated as accurately recorded details of natural phenomena.[91] In fact, they can be considered as Baconian "experiments."

As Jardine points out, the Renaissance did not, until Galileo introduced a new term for the purpose, differentiate between "experiment" and "experience"; hence "[a]ny observation illustrating some aspect of the topic under consideration which may prove useful in *deriving* a theory is an experiment . . . of *light*. . . . The great merit of experiments of light [as opposed to those of *fruit*, which yield some immediate practical benefit], according to Bacon, is that they are random observations, to no particular end, which therefore further investigation without in any way biasing it. . . ."[92]

Jardine's considered use of the word "observation," like Bacon's reference to Virgil's "observations of husbandry," is worth emphasizing here. The *OED* gives the following definition as being current since 1559: "The action or an act of observing scientifically a phenomenon in regard to its cause or effect, or phenomena in regard to their mutual relations, these being observed as

---

[90]Bacon uses the same figure ten pages earlier to introduce Parmenides' theory on the source of cold, "an opinion not to be despised" (V, 161; discussed above, p. 31).

[91]Such a case can be made even for what appears to be an off-handedly intruded metaphor (from *Aeneid* 4.173ff.) early in the *Historia ventorum*, in the midst of Bacon's suggestions for investigating the "progression" of winds:

Since progression always begins from a certain point, inquire as diligently as possible into the place of the first rising, and as it were the fountains of the winds. For winds appear to resemble Fame; which though they penetrate and bluster everywhere, yet hide their heads in the clouds. Inquire likewise into the progression itself. For instance, if a strong north wind blew on such a day or such an hour at York, did it blow two days afterwards in London? (*Works* V, 143–44)

Here, reversing the tenor and vehicle of Virgil's original metaphor (Fame resembles the winds), Bacon emphasizes the need for specific inquiry and observation regarding the origins, directions, and extent of winds.

[92]Jardine, 137–38, citing *Works*, IV, 95, 258. For Galileo's new term (*periculum*), see the studies by Charles B. Schmitt and P. Rief cited by Jardine, 137 n. 1; for the various kinds of natural histories identified by Bacon, see Jardine, 139.

they occur in nature." This meaning applies not only to the technical, "scientific" information in the *Georgics* (on field crops, trees
and the vine, weather-signs, farm animals, and bees). It also applies to the "testimony"—that is, to the accurate record of specific
natural observations—to be found as well in the *Eclogues* and
*Aeneid*, poems also written by one "by no means ignorant of natural philosophy." Such testimonies are therefore perfectly proper
in a Baconian natural history like the *Historia ventorum*.[93]

Similar appropriations of Virgilian "observations" are found in
the *Historia vitae et mortis* and the *Historia densi et rari*, the only
other natural histories—aside from *Sylva sylvarum*—which Bacon
developed beyond an introductory statement.[94] Three appear in
the first work (which contains many citations from ancient authors), two in the second (which has only a handful of citations
of any kind). In one instance, Virgil is mildly criticized for "following the common opinion" in *Georgics* 1.497 that men would
continue to decrease in stature as time passes (*Works*, V, 256), but
two other passages from Virgil's scientific poem are brought in as
supporting evidence for specific natural observations. In the *Historia vitae et mortis* Bacon says that "Virgil was right in speaking of
the use of casia as corrupting the use of clear oil" (*Works*, V, 286;
see *Georgics* 2.466), and in the *Historia densi et rari* Virgil is a witness as to the effects of extreme cold on bronze and cloth (V, 389;
see *Georgics* 3.363).

More striking, though, is the appearance of an identical passage from the *Eclogues* in both these natural histories. It is actually a simile from Alphesiboeus' anguished cry of love:

> limus ut hic durescit et haec ut cera liquescit
> uno eodemque igni, sic nostro Daphnis amore.

---

[93]While the focus here is on the natural histories, Bacon makes similar "testimonial"
appropriations of Virgil elsewhere. See, e.g., *Descriptio globi intellectualis* where, in a detailed discussion of celestial and meteorological phenomena, Bacon quotes *Georgics* 1.469–
71 to substantiate the "altered visage" of the sun in circumstances other than eclipses or
cloudy weather (*Works* V, 528–29); and *Advancement* where *Georgics* 1.250 is cited as evidence that the ancients knew of the antipodes (III, 340).

[94]*Sylva sylvarum* is Bacon's only "complete" natural history, but only because its struc-
ture is based not on nature but on a preconceived plan of ten topics, each with exactly one
hundred observations. Far from being "a just and perfect Natural History," Ellis points
out, this popular work is mainly a compilation of "facts . . . of which much the greater
part are taken from a few popular writers" (*Works*, II, 325), notably Giambattista della
Porta. For these reasons, I have not considered it in detail here, although the testimony of
Virgil is cited five times in the scientific way noted above; see II, 507, 536 (*Georgics*) and
502, 511, 642 (*Eclogues*). Given the fact that this posthumous work is the most "literary" of
the natural histories, it is ironic that Rawley concludes his preface with what he calls one
of Bacon's favorite sayings: "That this work of his Natural History is the world as God
made it, and not as men have made it; for that it hath nothing of imagination" (II, 337).

[As this clay hardens, and as this wax melts in one and the same flame, so may Daphnis melt with love for me!] (*Eclogues* 8.80–81, Loeb ed. and trans., pp. 60–61)

Of course Bacon leaves Daphnis out of it, but the powerful image clearly impressed him. For it is not only a case of a specific "observation" or "testimony" about clay and wax; it also embodies a general principle about the ability of heat to bring about contrary effects. In the *Historia vitae et mortis*, where it appears in the "History" of "Dessication," Bacon introduces it after paraphrasing its general import:

Fire and intense heat dry some things, but melt others. "In one and the same fire, clay grows hard and wax melts." Heat dries the earth, stones, wood, cloth, skins, and all bodies that cannot be melted. It melts metals, wax, gums, butter, tallow, and the like. (*Works*, V, 226–27)

Note how the quotation has the effect of *verifying* the generalization, and how Bacon repeats and then multiplies the examples of clay (earth) and wax.

In the *Historia densi et rari*, where the "Dilatations of bodies" as a result of heat is the subject, the quotation is used first as an example. The softening or melting of a body is "secret" and

takes place within the confines of the integral body, without visibly changing or increasing its bulk. But as soon as anything begins to escape in any body, then the actions become complicated, partly rarefying, partly contracting; so that those contrary actions of fire, which are commonly observed,

    As the same fire which makes the soft clay hard
    Makes hard wax soft,

are based on this; that in the one the spirit is emitted, in the other it is detained. (*Works*, V, 397)

On the next page, however, Bacon's list of "Provisional Rules" on density and rarity includes several that rephrase or refine upon Virgil's observation on the various effects of "the same fire":

14. Dense and rare are the proper effects of heat and cold; dense of heat, rare of cold.
15. Heat operates on pneumatic bodies by simple expansion.
16. Heat in a tangible body performs two operations; the pneumatic part it always dilates, but the gross part it sometimes contracts, sometimes relaxes.

17. Now the rule thereof is this; the emission of the spirit contracts and indurates the body; the detention of the spirit intenerates and melts it. (*Works*, V, 398)

In Bacon's natural histories, then, Virgil's "wit and learning" manifest themselves both in his accurate "observations" of specific natural phenomena and in more general observations, induced from those particulars.[95]

A fuller analysis of Bacon's deployment of Virgilian material might lead to further insights about Bacon's reading and appropriation of this "best poet." There is a suggestion, for example, in Jerry Weinberger's scrutiny of a crucial passage in the *Advancement* that the same passage from *Eclogues* 8 discussed above (a passage that clearly took hold of Bacon's imagination) may provide a key to the political and moral orientation of Bacon's "division of the sciences" into natural history, physics, and metaphysics.[96] In any case, the examples analyzed here demonstrate that for Bacon Virgil was, in the *Georgics*, a scientific poet in the tradition of Lucretius, and that even his mimetic poems contained the "wit and learning" of one who "was by no means ignorant of natural philosophy."

---

[95]Another instance of this can be seen in Bacon's allegorical exposition of Pan, where specific observations and general principles drawn from the *Eclogues* (2.63–64) enable Bacon to enunciate his entire scientific philosophy. Here Corydon's description of his own dogged pursuit of the disdainful Alexis becomes for Bacon an account of the chief activity of Pan and of the scientist:

Now the office of Pan can in no way be more lively set forth and explained than by calling him god of hunters. For every natural action, every motion and process of nature, is nothing else than a hunt. For the sciences and arts hunt after their works, human counsels hunt after their ends, and all things in nature hunt either after their food, which is like hunting for prey, or after their pleasures, which is like hunting for recreation;—and that too by methods skilful and sagacious.

After the wolf the lion steals; the wolf the kid doth follow;
The kid pursues the cytisus [clover] o'er hillock and thro' hollow. (*Works*, VI, 711)

(The Loeb trans. reads, "The grim lioness follows the wolf, the wolf himself the goat, the wanton goat the flowering clover, and Corydon follows you, Alexis. Each is led by his liking" [15]; note the generalization at the end.) Virgil has observed, in the particulars of animal behavior, a universal instinct which he applies to Corydon's desire for Alexis. Bacon, operating in a similar way, lists his own series of particular counterparts, each manifesting the universal (and abstract) law of nature that he is expounding in "Pan." This method is especially apt in the interpretation of myth or Parabolical Poesy, which in Bacon's definition is "typical History, by which [abstract] ideas that are objects of the intellect are represented in [concrete] forms that are objects of the sense" (see note 25, above).

[96]See *Advancement* (Works III, 354), *De augmentis* (IV, 346) and Weinberger's paraphrase and commentary in *Science, Faith, and Politics*, 246–47, 254–59.

# VI. CONCLUSION: POETIC LANGUAGE AND SCIENTIFIC DISCOURSE

The inconsistencies and contradictions in Bacon's poetic theory, as we saw in Part II, were one price he paid to keep Reason on top in his epistemological hierarchy. In order to demote Poesy to mere "fiction" and to reserve "rational" discourse for Philosophy, he adopts Aristotle's already inadequate criterion of mimesis as a definition for Poesy. In this and in refusing to confront the implications of didactic and scientific poetry, Bacon redefines in his own terms the "ancient quarrel between philosophy and poetry" and thereby perpetuates the muddle bequeathed by the Stagirite. In his practical writing on the philosophy of science, however, Bacon's frequent recourse to the Presocratic philosopher-poets, and especially to Lucretius, is a tacit recognition that the discursive scientific poetry of the ancients was a valuable source of scientific ideas, and his identification of Virgil's *Georgics* as another such poem is an unguarded acknowledgment—despite his formal poetic theory—of the whole tradition going back to Hesiod. Further erosion of Bacon's *a priori* categories of Reason and Imagination occurs in his unproblematized appropriation of what was for him the "experimental" observations and general scientific principles embedded in the mimetic poems of Virgil. These unresolved conflicts—both within his epistemological and poetic theory, and between theory and practice—are in large measure products of the very enterprise Bacon was undertaking: the articulation of a "new" mode of perceiving the world, while still burdened with the conceptual and linguistic baggage of the "old." Bacon was of course aware of this problem—just as he acknowledged that the Idols of the Marketplace (language) could not be wholly eradicated—but he was overly optimistic about its solution.

Over twenty years ago, Brian Vickers's stylistic analysis led him to characterize Bacon as a "thinker in images" whose "fundamentally analogous thinking" rendered him "not really a 'new man,' but an old-fashioned Renaissance mind."[97] More recently, disjunctions in his style and thought have been seen, via deconstruction, as the result of his failure to acknowledge the textuality of all discourse, even the most "objective" of "scientific reports." Hence, according to Charles Whitney, Bacon projected an unrealistic goal. He attempted to "naturalize the powers of tradition in the scientific enterprise"—that is, he adopted stylistic eloquence, poetic similitudes, and "cultivated" language generally as "instruments" for *presenting* his new scientific program (especially to a wider audience)—at the same time that he insisted that "the sons of science" should use a wholly "style-less" language for the expression of "objective scientific truth." This ideal (which we discussed above in relation to Bacon's natural histories), Whitney suggests, "set impossible standards for such control of traditional materials from the completely independent vantage point that he claims to have achieved."[98] One body of such "traditional materials" not examined before in this light is the scientific poetry of the ancients and the Virgilian works that for Bacon were so rich in "eloquence, wit, and learning." In practice, these poems cannot be "controlled" in a wholly detached way, any more than Bacon can wholly disengage himself from the traditional literary culture that produced his mental habits.

Perhaps the best example of his dilemma, and one that provides a final Baconian perspective on scientific poetry, can be found in that elegant summation of his scientific philosophy, the myth of Pan. Here, paradoxically but characteristically, he employs the ancient literary vehicle of mythic allegoresis to articulate his ideal of a new, "transparent" language, capable of uttering the "voice of nature" itself. It is instructive to observe how the "traditional" and "literary" strategy of mythic exposition refuses, as it were, to be a mere "instrument," "controlled" by the argument it is meant to forward.

We have already seen how Bacon uses Lucretius' analogy between letters and atoms to show how insignificant are the "tinklings" of men's voices (i.e., philosophical systems) in comparison with the "voice of nature" (p. 36, above); and how Rawley claims on Bacon's behalf that *Sylva sylvarum* (for all its indebtedness to

---

[97] *Francis Bacon and Renaissance Prose*, 172–73.

[98] *Francis Bacon and Modernity*, 154; see Chap. 5 there for a full analysis of these issues.

ness to della Porta's *Magia naturalis* and the like) represents an unmediated linguistic expression of "the world as God made it, and not as men have made it; for that it hath nothing of imagination" (n. 94, above). As both these cases suggest, Bacon's ideal of hearing and then expressing "the voice of nature" actually requires not only the exclusion of "Imagination," but also the impossible task of escaping the language of "men" altogether. In his exposition of the fable of Pan, the mythic context allows him, momentarily at least, to transcend such human limitations, while his metaphorical strategies attempt, though unsuccessfully, to subsume the problems inherent in the ineluctable contingency of all human knowledge and writing.

"No amours, or at least very few," says Bacon, "are related of Pan; a strange thing in a crowd of gods so profusely amorous. It is only said of him that he was the lover of Echo, who was also esteemed his wife; and of one other nymph besides, named Syringa; with desire for whom he was inflamed by the revengeful anger of Cupid, whom he had not scrupled to challenge to the wrestling" (*De augmentis, Works*, IV, 319). The allegorical exegesis is as follows:

Lastly it is no marvel if no loves are attributed to Pan, besides his marriage with Echo. For the world enjoys itself, and in itself all things that are. Now he who is in love wants something; and where there is plenty of everything there is no room for want. The world therefore can have no loves, nor any want (being content with itself), unless it be of *discourse*. Such is the nymph Echo, a thing not substantial but only a voice; or if it be of the more exact and delicate kind, *Syringa*,—when the words and voices are regulated and modulated by numbers, whether poetical or oratorical. But it is well devised that of all words and voices Echo alone should be chosen for the world's wife; for that is the true philosophy which echoes most faithfully the voices of the world itself, and is written as it were at the world's own dictation; being nothing else than the image and reflexion thereof, to which it adds nothing of its own, but only iterates and gives it back.[99]

Behind this allegory of Echo and Syringa stands the Reason-Imagination dichotomy with which we began. Echo is the impersonal, objective, unmediated, and rational discourse of science.

---

[99]*Works*, IV, 326-27. See Whitney's comment on this passage, 128-30; I agree generally with his interpretation of Echo, but my view of Syringa, the more problematical figure, differs considerably. A telling analogue for Bacon's allegory of Echo is in *Eclogues* 10.8, which he cites in *Advancement* and *De augmentis* in a similar way (*Works*, III, 363; IV, 371).

As Pan's "esteemed . . . wife" she is clearly contrasted with Syringa, for whom Pan (not usually "amorous") was "inflamed" with "desire . . . by revengeful anger": lawful (reasonable) love, as against unlawful and irrational passion. Though not stressed in the exegesis, these details from the description of Pan function subliminally to color the logical distinctions between Echo and Syringa which Bacon develops overtly—to the advantage of Echo.

In the exegesis itself, however, there are hints that what Echo stands for is only an unattainable dream, rather than a practically useful paradigm for human discourse. For Bacon cannot really define Echo herself in any pragmatically meaningful terms. This *"discourse"* is "not substantial but only a voice"; at the same time it is "faithfully . . . *written,* as it were at the world's own dictation." But rather than explain how human language can achieve this paradox of unsubstantial writing, he abruptly switches to a non-verbal metaphor which evades the question altogether: "being nothing else than the image and reflexion thereof, to which it adds nothing of its own, but only iterates and gives it back." Given his assertion elsewhere that "the mind of man" itself "is like an enchanted glass" (*Works,* III, 394–95), this diverting strategy of the mirror metaphor has its own drawbacks. Echo, then, remains an undefined and therefore unachievable ideal. Not surprisingly, Bacon cannot find an unmediated language to express the nature of a superhuman, wholly "transparent" language. He must rely on metaphor, with all its suggestive ambiguity and contextuality.[100]

When it comes to Syringa, "the more exact and delicate kind" of discourse," Bacon's language again fails him. Part of Syringa's meaning has to be inferred from what Echo is not. Presumably, Syringian discourse *does* add "[some]thing of its own," and presumably this is *style* since "the words and voices are regulated and modulated by numbers, whether oratorical or poetical." By making "the words and voices" plural, Bacon may be suggesting a contrast between the "many" and the one "true philosophy" of Echo. But *"the* words and voices" of Syringa's discourse are nevertheless those of Pan, to which the "regulated and modulated

---

[100]According to Whitney, these qualities are precisely what poetry "stands for" in Bacon's mind and what he is trying to denigrate through Syringa herself; see *Francis Bacon and Modernity,* 129–30. While Bacon chose to leave out the metamorphosis of Syringa into a reed and Pan's subsequent making of the Pan-pipes (Syrinx, named after her), this familiar story and its associations (Syringa as a figure for song and poetry) could not have been far from his mind; I am grateful to Anthony Low for this point.

numbers" of oratory or poetry have been added. It may appear,
as Whitney suggests, that these phrases mean simply "the already contextualized, Syringian world . . . of texts" (p. 130). But
note how literal and specific the technical references to prosody
and prose rhythm are, in contrast to the vague, mixed metaphors
describing Echo's discourse. As well as characterizing the general
*mode* of mediated discourse, that is, the Syringian categories of
"words and voices . . . regulated and modulated by numbers,
whether oratorical or poetical" denote actual, existing *genres* of
practical scientific writing. In fact, it is difficult not to identify
them respectively as "rhetorically expressed scientific prose" and
"scientific poetry."

That the second category refers to the kind of scientific poetry
we have been discussing seems clear. First, what else could the
"discourse" of nature regulated by poetical numbers be but discursive poetry on the nature of the universe, like that of Empedocles or Lucretius? Second, Bacon's reference to poetical *numbers*
indicates that here he is thinking neither of his reductive definition of Poesy as mimesis, nor of his usual denigrating metaphor
of "poetry" as standing for the vain words or matter of philosophical systems, the "poetry" of the Imagination's "philosophical theatre." On the contrary, Syringa does not create "fictions" of
any sort. That role is filled, in Bacon's allegory of Pan, by his
putative daughter, Iambe. She is "a little handmaid . . . who
used to amuse strangers with *ridiculous stories* . . . supposed by
some to be Pan's daughter by his wife Echo"; she represents
"those *vain babbling doctrines* about the nature of things, which
wander abroad in all times and fill the world; *doctrines barren in
fact, counterfeit in breed*, but by reason of their garrulity sometimes
entertaining, and sometimes again troublesome and annoying."[101]
Therefore, the Syringian discourse that is metrically regulated is
an actual form of human writing capable of communicating the
"voices of nature," without descending into the fictions of false
philosophy. Discursive scientific poetry, that is, while it may
share the imperfections (i.e., the inherent referentiality) of discursive scientific prose, has as much validity; both are human
expressions of human knowledge.

However much Bacon may wish to dismiss both these kinds of
Syringian discourse in favor of the idealized, unmediated "voice"

[101]*Works*, IV, 319, 327; emphasis added. For the typical pairing of poetry with the vain
philosophy of the "philosophical theatres," see Farrington, 41–42, 69, 84–85, 87; and
*Novum Organum, Works*, IV, 63.

of Echo, the logic of his own mythic exegesis seems to grant a reluctant acknowledgment that attaining the latter is impossible. As well, it suggests, almost in spite of itself, the necessity of accepting Syringa, if only because her discourse in effect describes all actual scientific discourse: even a "style-less" prose has "style." This can be seen again in the ambiguities of the very language meant to put Syringa in her place. Her discourse is confusingly described in terms that are, potentially at least, both positive and negative: it is "of the more exact and delicate kind." In the *Advancement*, "delicate learning"—"where men study words and not matter"—is of course the first of three "distempers" that have most discredited learning (*Works*, III, 282–285). Here, Bacon seems to apply this potentially pejorative term to the "voices [that] are . . . modulated by [oratorical] numbers" and thereby suggest that Syringian discourse is characterized by the same kind of excesses found in Ciceronian style. (The linkage of "voices . . . modulated . . . numbers" may also entail musical associations, suggesting further stylistic "additions"—frivolous and unnecessary—by Syringa.) The placing of "exact," on the other hand, suggests that it applies to "words . . . regulated . . . by [poetical] numbers." This perhaps recalls Bacon's initial definition of Poesy in *De augmentis* as "a part of learning in measure of words for the most part restrained." In that context the restrained "measure of words" is a kind of minimal virtue, a tiny saving grace, played off against the fact that "in all other points [Poesy is] extremely free and licensed" (*Works*, IV, 314–315). In the present context, however, "exact" maintains its positive force, and even "delicate" lacks the barbs of its usage in the *Advancement*. We are left with the confusion that however "faithfully" Echo "iterates" the "world's own dictation," Syringa's discourse of nature is "more exact and delicate."[102]

Bacon's account of Echo and Syringa, then, exemplifies the very problem of human language it is meant to expose and eliminate. Furthermore, the ambiguities and confusions here recall those of his epistemology and poetic theory—and not just fortuitously. As we saw, Echo and Syringa are subtly associated with Reason and Imagination, and Bacon's efforts (logical and verbal) to valorize one at the expense of the other are quite similar, as are their failures. Bacon's identification of scientific poetry as one kind of Syringian discourse, and the implied acceptance of that

---

[102]The Latin version gives only *accuratiores* (*Works*, I, 530), which can mean both "more exact, more carefully prepared," and "more studied, elaborate."

discourse as generally equivalent to all human (i.e., mediated) scientific communication, have their counterparts in his own appropriations of ancient scientific poetry (including the *Georgics*, which he unguardedly identifies as such) and in the Syringian mode of his own scientific writing.

A broader perspective on Bacon's engagement with ancient scientific poetry—which historians of science might still be tempted to dismiss as the literary attachment of one who did not actually engage in "hard" scientific activity—is provided by a recent study of early seventeenth-century atomism. Christoph Meinel has shown that for those atomists who were empiricists—"in [whose] systems the clearest departure from merely bookish reasoning could be expected"—it was not scientific experiments (Galileo's *pericula*) but vivid passages from Lucretius' *De rerum natura* (Baconian *experientiae*) that gave the strongest "proofs" for this newly revived theory of matter.[103] Meinel demonstrates that there are Lucretian precedents for each of the six categories of empirical arguments in favor of corpuscularianism in this period: "In almost all of these cases the experiences [i.e., observations] referred to were little more than variations on classical themes. Even when true experiments were carried out, they were often merely practical performances from a common repertory of literary [primarily Lucretian] paradigms" (p. 101). Along with the application of the microscope and the technological pragmatism of metallurgists and chemists, the most powerful lines of argument came from "the pervasive appeal of the pictorial scheme supplied by Lucretius' poetic imagery, which offered an immediately convincing way of picturing material processes on the basis of everyday experience within the visible world" (p. 103).

It is ironic, though, that even so astute a historian as Meinel can write as though the scientific discourse of these empiricists were a pre-existent or utterly self-contained mode—one capable of contamination by extrinsic "rhetorical" or "fictional" elements—and not one (as Bacon himself recognized) that had to be painfully created. He expresses astonishment, for example, that Lucretian arguments for the invisible movement of matter (as in evaporation or the imperceptible wearing down of tools or stone

---

[103]Christoph Meinel, "Early Seventeenth-Century Atomism: Theory, Epistemology, and the Insufficiency of Experiment," *Isis* 79 (1988): 68–103; quotation from 69.

steps) could be taken seriously by empiricists, some of whom actually constructed experiments to prove them:

> the frequent occurrence and repetition of these observations, the pervasive idea that truth should be visible or could be thought of in a pictorial way, *infiltrated scholarly discourse and the very language of science.* Atomism was an enticingly pictorial image of reality. The wealth of appealing and immediately convincing images offered by Lucretius's poem supplied the scheme according to which material change was assumed to occur in nature. (p. 85, emphasis added).

Given Bacon's realization that the Idols of the Market-place are here to stay, and given his general failure to disentangle himself from Syringian discourse—*in spite of* a self-conscious effort to do so, and to imagine a language that could serenely "echo" objective scientific truth—we should rather be surprised that Lucretius and other Syringian voices are not *more* prominent in the "very language of science" of Bacon's empiricist contemporaries, who did not grapple self-reflexively with these questions. The final irony in all this is that the power of Lucretius' poem over philosopher of science and empiricists alike is almost certainly the result of a calculated poetic strategy of creating "clear images" by which to present the invisible through the sensible.[104]

While Bacon would be unable to accept consciously the kind of scientific exactitude that Lucretius claimed for Empedocles' poetry and for his own (see n. 3, above), it is clear that the "more exact and delicate" discourse of ancient scientific poetry—along with the mimetic poems of Virgil, laden with "wit and

---

[104]"Lucretius presents us with a poem which represents the order or *ratio* of nature in the arrangement of its letters, sounds, words, arguments and images and which at the same time can claim to be ordered according to the *species* of nature, because it presents images and arguments which are perceived like the *simulacra* of things. It appears that Lucretius' images and his arguments are properly aligned and connected with respect to each other and to external reality, so that the *De Rerum Natura* is truly a representation of reality which fulfills Lucretius' intention as stated just after the proemium of Book 1:
  Hunc igitur terrorem animi tenebrasque necessest / non radii solis neque lucida tela diei / discutiant, sed naturae species ratioque. ['This terror of mind therefore and this gloom must be dispelled, not by the sun's rays or the bright shafts of day, but by the aspect and law of nature' (Loeb trans., 1.146–48).]"
See the full argument behind these conclusions, in Eva M. Thury, "Lucretius' Poem as a *Simulacrum* of the *Rerum Natura*," *American Journal of Philology* 108 (1987): 270–94; quotation from 292.

learning"—exerted a remarkable influence on his scientific philosophy: not just in the imagery of its expression, but in the formation of some of his most important ideas. This is not to say, with Shelley, that Bacon was a "poet," but that like the greatest scientific discoverers—Faraday, Kekulé, Einstein—Bacon could not divorce reason and imagination.[105]

---

[105] I am thinking of Faraday's hallucinations of the "lines of force" surrounding magnets and of Kekulé's vision of the benzene ring in the Gnostic and alchemical symbol of the ouroboros serpent. For Einstein, "the words of the language as they are written or spoken do not seem to play any role in my mechanism of thought . . . which relies on more or less clear images of a visual and some of a muscular type." Note how similar these instances are to the Lucretius' "pictorial image[s] of reality" presented as "unscientific" by Meinel. For accounts of these three scientists, see John Read, *Prelude to Chemistry: An Outline of Alchemy* (1936; Cambridge, Mass.: M.I.T. Press, 1966), 241; and Arthur Koestler, *Janus: A Summing Up* (1978; London: Pan, 1983), 149–51, and 155–56 for the complementarity of intuition and scientific thought.

# INDEX

Addison, Joseph, 8n16

Aetius, 39n69

Alchemical poetry, 26n39, 49n89

Anaxagoras, 2n3, 27n41, 34

Aratus, 3n6, 24, 45n80

Aristotle, 9n19, 34n56, 4n71; ambivalence toward Empedocles as poet, 1-2, 4, 42; contradictions in poetic theory, 1-3, 54; identifies Empedocles with theory of four elements, 32; and the "nameless genres," 24n36; his scientific speculations rejected by Bacon, 9, 30-31, 33; theory of imagination, 17-18

Astrological poetry, 26n39, 49n89

Avienus (translator of Aratus), 3n6

Bacon, Francis: disjunction between his style and thought, 54-55; "georgics of the mind," 46; ideal of unmediated language, 9, 54-60
—epistemology: classification of human learning, 11; imagination as faculty producing poesy, 11-12; imagination (poesy) inferior to reason (philosophy), 11-24; contradictions in his theory of imagination, 14-24, 43, 54-56; theory of imagination differs from Aristotle's, 17-18; memory as faculty producing history, 11-12; the "pyramid" of knowledge, 12-13, 29; reason as highest faculty, producing philosophy (science), 11-12
—mythography (parabolical poesy), 4n8, 10n20, 14n25, 20n33, 25n40, 32, 45n82
—myths, scientific allegories of: Coelum, 34-35; Cupid, 29-30, 40-41; Pan, 53n93, 55-60
—poetic theory, 9-10, 11-24; classification of genres, 20-24; how like Sidney's, 15, 20n33; scientific poetry excluded from, 20-24, 42
—poetry: distinguished from history, 13; superior to history, 14-15; as product of imagination, 12, 14-24; as fiction, 12-13; as irrational, 15-18; verse form not essential to, 20-22; verse form in relation to specific genres of, 21-23
—works: Advancement, 13n23, 15n27, 1n30, 25n38, 27nn40, 42; 28, 35n60, 42, 45n82, 46, 47, 51n93, 53n96, 56n99, 59; Cogitata et visa, 35n60; Cogitationes de natura rerum, 35-37; De augmentis, 11-23, 25n38, 27n40, 28, 29, 38n65, 41n72, 43-45, 46, 53n96, 56n99, 59; De principiis,

29-31, 33, 35, 40-41; Descriptio globi intellectualis, 13n24, 33, 38-40, 51n93; Essays, 42; Historia densi et rari, 51-53; Historia ventorum, 26n39, 31, 47-51; Historia vitae et mortis, 27, 28, 32, 51, 52; New Atlantis, 13n23; Novum organum, 13n23, 15n17, 17, 18n30, 25n38, 26n40, 28, 32, 33, 35n61, 37n64, 42, 58n101; Parasceve, 48; Redargutio philosophorum, 25n38, 27, 35n60; Sylva sylvarum, 32n49, 40n71, 51, 55-56; Thema coeli, 29; Wisdom of the Ancients, 25n38, 26n40, 29, 32, 34, 43-45, 53n95

Beni, Paolo, 6

Bruni, Leonardo, 5n10

Buchanan, George, 5n9

Callimachus, 6

Campanella, Tommaso, 11n21

Capriano, G. P., 6

Cardano, Geronimo, 11n21

Carew, Richard, 11n21

Carpenter, Nathaniel, 25n37

Castelvetro, Ludovico, 6, 19n31

Chapman, George, 46n84

Cicero, 3n6, 5, 6, 9n19

Clement of Alexandria, 27n42

Cocking, John M., 17

Columella, 3n6

Crates of Mallos, 6

Dante, 5

Democritus, 27, 28, 29, 34; his atomic theory favored by Bacon, 9; his atomic theory found in Lucretius by Bacon, 27, 35-41; his atomic theory expounded in Bacon's mythography, 34-35, 43-45; his materialism preferred by Bacon over Plato's idealism, 26; most important Presocratic for Bacon, 26; his theory of vacuum reconstituted from Lucretius by Bacon, 38-39

Didactic poetry. See Lehrgedicht; Poetry; Scientific poetry

Diogenes Laertius, 9n19, 27n42, 32n50, 39n69

Dolce, Ludovico, 5

Dryden, John, 8n16

Du Bartas, Guillaume de Salluste, 26n39

Einstein, Albert, 62

Empedocles: compared to Homer, 2, 5, 12; influence on Georgics, 45n80; and Parmenides, 9, 32n50; as poet, not versifier of science, 2-3; not a genuine poet according to Aristotle, 1-2; according to Capriano, 6; not

www.ingramcontent.com/pod-product-compliance
Lightning Source LLC
Chambersburg PA
CBHW050350110426
42812CB00008B/2424